John Costello

The Pocket Essential

WRITING A SCREENPLAY

First published in Great Britain 2002 by Pocket Essentials, 18 Coleswood Road, Harpenden, Herts, AL5 1EQ

Distributed in the USA by Trafalgar Square Publishing, PO Box 257, Howe Hill Road, North Pomfret, Vermont 05053

A CIP catalogue record for this book is available from the British Library.

ISBN 1-903047-47-1

4 6 8 10 9 7 5 3

Book typeset by Wordsmith Solutions Ltd
Printed and bound by Cox & Wyman

Placebo, Unkle, Or
Rammstein, Covenant,
the Holy Trinity - Magma,

204 306

01603 773114
email: tis@ccn.ac.uk

21 DAY LOAN ITEM

2 5 FEB 2019

CONTENTS

FADE OUT.

"Photography is truth. Cinema is truth 24 times per second."

Jean-Luc Godard (Writer/Director)

"I believe you need to write a million words of crap before you get it right."

Simon Moore (Screenwriter)

"A professional writer is an amateur who didn't quit."

Richard Bach (Writer)

1. FADE IN:

"Writing a screenplay is like climbing a mountain. When you're climbing, all you can see is the rock in front of you and the rock directly above you. You can't see where you've come from or where you're going."

Syd Field (Screenwriting Lecturer)

Introduction

This book is about the labour of love that is writing a screenplay. It is aimed at the beginner (although I hope writers of all levels will find it useful), so it is simple, straightforward and easy to use. Each stage of the screenwriting process is covered, from generating and developing ideas to selling the finished product. Jargon is kept to a minimum, complex and confusing graphs, flow charts, tables and diagrams are avoided, and a useful glossary of terms is included. If your goal is to write for television, you should still find plenty of interest here, but the emphasis is firmly on writing for the feature film market.

Although I am honoured to write about a subject so close to my heart, deciding what to exclude has been agonizing. Five hundred pages would have been a cinch; a hundred has been a nightmare; not dissimilar to the screenwriting process itself. Screenwriting uses a minimum of words to convey the maximum emotion to the reader. In a feature film script, the writer has 100-120 pages of mainly white paper to engage and sustain interest; to take the reader on an exhilarating journey they won't want to end.

Inevitably, as well as being informative and, I hope, entertaining, this book includes my observations and opinions on the screenwriting process, the industry market place and the quality of certain films. I have tried to give reasons and back up arguments, but feel free to disagree, to speculate about my parentage and fling the book across the room if you wish. That's the beauty of subjectivity. Your opinion and mine may both be intelligent, informed and considered, yet for all that they may still be poles apart. Everyone has their own individual likes, dislikes, tastes and reasons. There are no absolutes in the film industry. No guarantees, no sure-fire winners, no projects immune from disaster, only opinions. As William Goldman so astutely put it in *Adventures In The Screen Trade*: 'NOBODY KNOWS ANYTHING.'

Therefore, allow me to share a few of my suspicions...

Backstory

Whether or not it is possible to teach the *art* of writing, I sincerely believe that it is possible to teach the *craft*. I have taught screenwriting classes at the University Of Warwick for five years, mainly to beginners with little or no experience of the form. I have also lectured on the Screenwriting MA at Sheffield University and I am currently preparing the Screenwriting module for Birmingham University's Creative Writing BA. Some of my students have sold work to film and TV markets, some have written and directed short films, some have even won awards.

During those five years I have read many, many scripts. A handful were good, a few very good, but none were *great*. The vast majority ranged from poor to awful. If I were a producer looking to make a return on my money, I would have gambled on two, maybe three. The overall standard of speculative (i.e. non-commissioned) scripts in the UK is not high. Criminally, some writers just don't bother to learn the craft and 'rules' of screenwriting (or worse, refuse, or worse still, reject them outright), yet still expect to be taken seriously.

Spec scripts in the USA are generally better, as you might expect. The reasons for this are varied and complex, but one can point to certain differences of culture, temperament and storytelling style between US and UK writers. Screenwriting substitutes for religion in LA; novices don't exist. Waiters and bellhops are born with ink in their veins. American screenwriters don't view 'entertainment' as a pejorative term. For me though, the key factor is the differing emphasis placed in the respective markets on developing a cinematic sensibility.

Cinematic Vs. Televisual

Scenario A: You focus on a strong central character with clearly defined goals, needs and problems. You tell your story primarily through actions and visuals. Your canvas is broad; your milieu intriguing and expansive. Your theme reaches out to the reader's humanity. There is something new and fresh about your work. You have something different to say.

Scenario B: You sketch a bunch of frequently selfish and/or irritating characters with a catalogue of problems and a lot to say for themselves; to misappropriate the title of a Philip K Dick novel, *Puttering About In A Small Land*. You tell your story primarily through dialogue. Your milieu is overfamiliar and restricted. Your premise suffers from a lack of theme, or your theme panders to negative emotions. There's nothing original here; we've seen it all before. You simply need to keep money coming in.

Many writers who instinctively place themselves in Scenario A are mistaken. Decide for yourself, *objectively*. If you do belong in A, your material is cinematic and stands a good chance of success. If you are closer to B, your material is televisual, and needs to improve whether you are writing for film or television. The majority of scripts I read are in fact bland television masquerading as film. This stems from their lack of cinematic characteristics: originality, breadth, style, ambition, action, consistency, clarity of vision and mastery of dramatic structure.

We live in a TV-dominated culture but unfortunately the dearth of good writing for television creates a mediocrity-go-round for writers. Of course, the best TV writing remains excellent (*The Sopranos, Queer As Folk, The Office, 24, The West Wing, Six Feet Under*) and the worst film writing remains abysmal, whether targeting a puerile, undemanding teen market (*Booty Call, Pootie Tang, Dude, Where's My Car, The Animal*), no discernible market at all (a huge problem with British films) or following a shameless, soulless fast-food formula (*Planet Of The Apes* remake, *Gone In 60 Seconds* remake, *Tomb Raider, End Of Days*). That such material is commissioned and produced betrays an inherently flawed system on both sides of the pond; after all, writers must obey the demands of the market place if they want to eat. The US market largely recycles cynical lowest-common-denominator fodder: endless remakes, sequels and computer game or comic adaptations. The UK market largely recycles popular televisual mediocrity *which simply does not translate to the big screen*. Ironically, the more US television becomes cinematic, the more UK cinema becomes televisual; not an ideal situation.

The worst American films tend to be in the aforementioned teen market, but at least it's a lucrative one; much Hollywood product is aimed at 15-year-old males because they visit the cinema most often and spend the most on confectionery. With British films, however, it's hard to discern which market they are aimed at. Behind every *The Full Monty* or *Four Weddings And A Funeral* or *Billy Elliot* there follows a legion of lead caskets to strike fear into the hearts of even the most dynamic PR hypers: *Guest House Paradiso, Circus, Honest, Saving Grace, Rancid Aluminium, The Designated Mourner, Fanny & Elvis, Essex Boys, Sorted, Dad Savage, Nora, Purely Belter, Amy Foster, A Room For Romeo Brass, Mad Cows, Bring Me The Head Of Mavis Davis, Maybe Baby, Very Annie Mary, The Martins, Mike Bassett: England Manager, Janice Beard 45 WPM*.

I make no apologies for holding a general antipathy towards the underachieving, unambitious culture of British films; as I said, this is my subjective opinion, savage it at your leisure. It's my contention that the majority of American films are superior, at the heart of which lies their cinematic identity - derived from the fact that American writers, particularly in the vibrant independent sector, have researched the market place, studied the sophisticated storytelling and stylistic techniques of the best film-makers in the world, *and have incorporated them into their own work*. Few British writers do this. In *The Guerilla Film Makers Handbook*, James Wilson, Deputy Head of Production at Film Four, says of the British film industry: "I despair of a film culture that can't think beyond the stylistic language of *Eastenders*. Film is its own language, not an extension of the language of TV drama or theatre. It's about having a strong voice, whether it's *Happiness*, *The Idiots*, or *Being John Malkovich*. Who's got voices like those in the UK? Who's got the balls?" Who indeed?

An off-the-cuff list of excellent recent American films: *The Insider*, *Requiem For A Dream*, *Being John Malkovich*, *Three Kings*, *Go*, *Almost Famous*, *Happiness*, *American History X*, *The Limey*, *The Straight Story*, *Fight Club*, *The Iron Giant*, *Your Friends And Neighbors*, *Buffalo 66*, *American Beauty*, *Magnolia*, *The Matrix*, *Wonder Boys*, *The Virgin Suicides*, *Traffic*. I could mention many more. Excellent examples of recent world cinema include: *Run Lola Run* (Germany), *La Veuve De Saint Pierre* and *Amélie* (France), *All About My Mother* and *Open Your Eyes* (Spain), *Last Night* (Canada), *Cure: The Power Of Suggestion* and *Battle Royale* (Japan), *Together* (Sweden), *Amores Perros* (Mexico), *Our Lady Of The Assassins* (Colombia), *The Dish* (Australia), *Funny Games* (Austria) and countless others. Excellent recent British films: *East Is East*, *Wonderland*, *Memento*, *Croupier*, *Sexy Beast*. Five films, of which the first two are really television. I couldn't think of others, and therein lies the problem.

So if the situation is so bad, why bother at all? Well, because when we see a great film there are few experiences to touch it. The thought of writing a film which electrifies the emotions of a large audience should be motivation enough. If you aspire to write a screenplay with viable commercial prospects in a diminished and devalued market place, *and* an aesthetic weight you can be proud of, you're aiming for a goal that few British screenwriters currently achieve, or in truth even set themselves. Watch *American Beauty*, *The Dish* and *All About My Mother* for examples of how intimate character drama can still attain a cinematic gravitas. And the next time you pay to see yet another disappointing film that fails to engage you and would lose nothing on your portable TV screen, channel your emotion into creating something better yourself; something genuinely cinematic, something to (please) prove me wrong.

Spoiler Warning

It goes against all of my instincts to give away key film twists, switches, shocks, reveals and endings... but in this book it's an occupational hazard and I'm afraid I do. All the time.

On The Road

After reading this book, you should understand a great deal more about the art and craft of screenwriting, the conventions of narrative, the importance of character and structure, the necessity of adhering to screenplay format and the sheer magnitude of the task of writing a great *visual* script. I hope you will also feel galvanised and better equipped to tackle this task. This book provides help and advice on writing an original, entertaining screenplay, *if* you're prepared to put your heart and soul into it. Time to find out...

2. Motivation & Ideas

"Writing is a personal responsibility"

Syd Field (Screenwriting Lecturer)

Motivation

What drives us to write? A spiritual desire to create art, or a more prosaic need to pay the bills? Whatever the reason, the act of writing demands discipline, effort, commitment and, perhaps above all, motivation. Motivation is the x factor that drives you to sit in front of the computer and move your fingers every day, no matter how much you hate the thought and no matter how badly things are going. If you lose motivation, writing becomes a chore and before long all those odd jobs that you'd put off for years start getting done. You're only too happy to decorate or mend the shed or wash the car. Daytime television takes on a strange allure. Anything to avoid staring at the damn computer.

Writing a screenplay, whether destined to put an Oscar on your mantel or to line a litter tray, requires regular hard work towards goals of self-improvement and sales, and involves careful planning, research and execution. Neglect any of these areas at your peril. The best way to build your confidence and improve as a writer is to plan regularly, research regularly and write regularly. Or, to put it more simply, wise up and adopt a professional attitude.

The chief obstacle to motivation is fear: fear of groping around in the dark; fear of not being good enough; fear of embarrassment, defeat, failure. One of the aims of this book is to provide the knowledge you'll need to conquer your fear and motivate yourself, allowing you to write with confidence and produce higher quality material.

Finding Your Voice

The prospects of fortune and success in a glamorous industry certainly provide incentives for screenwriters, but don't become sidetracked from the writer's greatest motivation of all: finding something you just have to say; something that makes you lick your lips in anticipation of booting up the computer every day.

Finding your voice is a tricky concept to explain. It's a combination of saying what you want to say, in the way you want to say it, and developing an ability to say it with an originality and flair that makes the combination special. To succeed, your work needs a consistency of vision and a style of execution that elevates it above the average. It should show you in the best possible light; as a creative artist who is professional enough to learn and employ the craft of screenwriting.

Unfortunately, finding your voice is, like everything else, a process - it doesn't happen spontaneously. Don't be surprised when your first efforts appal you and bear little resemblance to what you want to say, or how. It's that way for most of us. Don't become demotivated and give up because quality can only be arrived at via quantity. If you realise this, you'll be able to expel your initial garbage and write past it. Remember - nothing good is written, it's always *re*written.

Another obstacle is that the prospect of revealing one's innermost idiosyncrasies is often acutely embarrassing. But it is precisely this quality that the industry is looking for - a new voice with something different to say, and a fresh, individual way of saying it. Far too many writers hide their real voices behind façades of structure and plot, leaving their work empty and formulaic. Write your individuality onto the page. I would rather read a flawed script with personality shining through than a technically proficient but soulless script. The former can be remedied; the latter usually cannot.

Art Vs. Craft

It's dangerous for a screenwriter to view himself solely as an artist. A talented student once told me, "I don't need to learn structure - I want to write a film, not a movie." He never completed a first draft. If you share this highbrow self-image, maybe you should consider other forms of expression: painting, sculpture, novels or poetry. I'm certainly not denigrating such endeavours, but screenwriting is a synergy of craft and art, in that order. It allows plenty of room for creativity - within the parameters of a flexible structure and inflexible format. First learn the craft and then supply the talent because (unless you are truly exceptional) without the artifice the art will not be enough.

Discipline

If your embryonic writing projects are legion, all once promising but now discarded, or you make good progress until you reach the final straight, you are fleeing the most basic discipline of writing - Finish What You Start. For most of us the reality is that little comes easily. Hard work, hard thought and hard choices are the order of the day, every day. To break through this mental barrier you must develop a disciplined approach that treats writing as the bedrock of your daily life.

One obstacle is that writing sometimes doesn't really feel like work. It's so easy to duck out of. You're at home so you can watch TV, get a sandwich, send emails, whatever. Train yourself to treat writing as a *job*. If you can't write at home, find office space. If you have a full-time occupation, then writing becomes your part-time one. If you don't, then write nine-to-five, or if you're a night owl, nine pm to five am. You alone can decide how much time you can afford. Tuck the writing in comfortably around your commitments, or vice-versa. But be prepared for the possibility that if you simply can't spare enough time and/or energy, or after months you'd still rather have an enema than turn on the computer then, like anything in life, if you can't enjoy it you'd probably be better off doing something else. As Quentin Crisp put it, "If at first you don't succeed, then darling, failure may be your forte."

Routine

Art Arthurs' phrase "Seat of the pants to the seat of the chair" is one of the most motivating mantras I know. I often say it aloud when I'm tempted back to the TV, DVD or CD; it reminds me that the only way to finish what I start is to sit and graft every day. Also, I find writing so much easier when I exercise my brain regularly. Upon returning cold after a period of neglect (usually justified as a 'break'), even basic grammar and sentence construction is a struggle for around two days until it all flows again and I curse myself for the wasted time and effort my 'break' has cost.

It's all about routine. Discipline demands it and deadlines dictate it. In any job, people prefer to know in advance what they're expected to produce, and when. You should determine your own preferred routine once you've discovered your most productive writing time. Mine is at night, almost always with music and Mrs Daniels' son Jack for company. I have friends who can only work in silence, or with mineral water, or in two-hour bursts or who simply have to keep going until they've poured themselves out.

When establishing a routine, short-term goal setting is important. Without goals it is far easier to procrastinate, avoid or flee. Goals should be achievable without pushing yourself too hard. Simon Beaufoy, writer of *The Full Monty*, illustrates this: "What I mostly try and do is set myself about five pages a day to write, and of course that's a great theory but actually what happens is on a good day you'll write maybe ten pages, but mostly... you'll sit there and twiddle your thumbs and stare out the window and curse the world that you ever took on such a project."

When you're ready to write your first feature script draft, five pages a day will see it completed in around twenty working days. When put like that it some-how doesn't appear as daunting, does it? Just remember that it takes months of research and preparation to reach the draft stage.

One final point: it is important that if there are significant others in your life; partner, children etc, you should discuss your ambitions and your proposed routine with them, and make sure they understand that this is your private time and that you are deadly serious about it. If they are not with you on this it will cause problems. Weigh up the pros and cons. If your activities are reasonable, then go for it - if you don't do it now, you'll probably never do it.

For Whom Do You Write?

Something that comes as a revelation to many students is the concept that you write not for an audience, or the director, or yourself but for the *reader*. Not only a script reader working for a production company but any reader that sits down with your screenplay at any time.

People who turn to scriptwriting under the mistaken assumption that it is an easier literary form to master or to sell than a novel couldn't be more wrong. The attraction is easy to see: novels run to hundreds of pages, while screenplay length is 90-120 pages. Novels maximise, screenplays minimise. Novels tell stories through language, screenplays through visuals. However, the principle of learning the form before trying to produce your best work in it remains the same. You should write with a potential audience in mind but your words must succeed in their own right; they must come alive on the page and entertain anyone who reads them. The fruit of any labour must be of the highest quality to succeed in its market place.

Script Readers

Once you submit your screenplay to production companies, it enters the domain of those mythical industry gatekeepers, the script readers. Their role is to provide written 'coverage' of your script. In *The Guerilla Film Makers Handbook*, a script reader describes the content of coverage: "...a brief 'logline' which sums up what the script is about in two or three sentences, a 'synopsis' of what happens in the script,... a 'comment' outlining what the script reader feels the script is trying to do, how well it does it, whether the premise is original and engaging, what could be done to improve it and the sort of audience it is likely to appeal to... Finally, a 'verdict' or 'recommendation' on the script will indicate whether it should be accepted, rejected or developed."

Readers' instincts are to find reasons to keep the writer out, for which they are often viewed with suspicion or hostility, but their instincts are based on experience - that this script, like the previous one and the one before that, will contain a host of deficiencies from the same predictable menu. Writers load their scripts with them, making the readers' job easy. Do all you can to ensure your script is dramatic, tense, funny, harrowing, touching, entertaining, emotional, *different*; the best art you can produce after researching the craft and the market. Razzle dazzle 'em - if you can make the gatekeepers laugh and cry, the doors to the inner sanctum will start to open for you.

Ideas

"The most embarrassing and shameful experiences of your life; the things you can hardly bear to think about, let alone tell anyone else; your secret dreams, your darkest desires: these are your core material."

Andrew Davies (Novelist/Screenwriter)

The Value Of Ideas

Ideas are your lifeblood. Without them, your writing will be of little interest to you or to anyone else. They can appear from out of the blue, day or night, and you must be prepared to capture, nurture and develop them. If you can do this, they become your best friends.

So what is the true value, in hard currency, of a great idea? Most students' eager replies to this question vary from "a few thousand pounds" to "several million dollars." They're often surprised to find that the answer is... absolutely nothing. Think about it. What would you say if a stranger approached you and said "I have a fabulous idea. How much will you pay me for it?" Well, that's what people in the film business say too. To update the old Hollywood axiom, ideas are a dime a dozen - and then factor in depreciation. It's always what you do with them that counts and that comes down to talent. If you're a great writer but your ideas are lousy, your script will be lousy, but you can find material to adapt. If your ideas are great but you're a lousy writer, your script will be lousy also, and you should consider collaborating with a good writer. Only if you can transform your best ideas into a marketable commodity - a screenplay that is your very best work, contains originality and style, entertains the reader, is carefully structured, features three-dimensional characters, memorable dialogue, is professionally presented using correct format and binding, with correct spelling, grammar and punctuation - then and only then does the prospect of financial reward enter the equation.

Every writer has different interests, likes and dislikes, and each should play to his own personality. French writer/director François Truffaut said "...20% of my material is autobiographical, 20% comes from newspapers, 20% from people I know and 20% is pure fiction. Fiction does not play a major part. I prefer to work from real life." In contrast, Truffaut fan and media sponge Quentin Tarantino assimilates (some might say plunders) many ideas from films, television, books, comics and other elements of popular culture. In his defence, he makes a virtue of this and wears his influences proudly on his sleeve. The inherent truth of the adage 'nothing new under the sun' means that writers who have the talent to put the most interesting and ingenious spins on old ideas will find an audience, and therefore a sale.

Inspiration

'5% inspiration, 95% perspiration' is a tired catchphrase... and also true. Inspiration is vital because without the 5%, the 95% cannot happen. You should cultivate a mindset receptive to inspiration by planning properly, researching thoroughly and writing regularly, thereby reducing your emotional stress and allowing you to think clearly. The more relaxed you are, the more inspired your ideas will become.

Don't expect miracles. Your fingers will seldom fly across the keys, spinning reams of golden words. Mostly, the order of the day is hard work, frustration, anger and self-doubt. Expect to spin 95% manure at first. Your persistence will afford you access to those moments of clarity and excitement more often, the intervals between moments of inspiration will become shorter and the moments themselves will elongate.

Generating Ideas

Like every part of the writing process, this is both discipline and duty. You have to train your mind to think visually, produce ideas in quantity, hold on to inspiration when it strikes, and search all your darkest, dankest corners. Recently I watched a TV documentary about cannibal killers, on which a psychologist described how a killer regarded fellow humans as "furniture." This gave me a new perspective on a character of mine - he kills because he simply does not see other people as 'human' - and a new working title. Here are a few tips:

- **What if..?** Most ideas can be boiled down to 'what if?' but try to hit the dramatic core: What if JFK really was assassinated by an FBI-led conspiracy? What if more-than-human off-world 'replicants' are loose on Earth and searching for their maker? What if the only man brilliant enough to find a clever serial killer is himself a cannibal serial killer in a high-security jail? What if, during the most important deal of his life, an East End crime boss has war brought to his doorstep by one of his closest aides' own disastrous side deal? What if an ordinary woman is hunted by a cyborg sent from the future to ensure that her unborn son never exists?

- **Stimuli.** A photograph, a poem, a piece of music (bizarrely, Luc Besson wrote *Nikita* in response to the Elton John song), a random stab into a book, anything that stimulates your imagination to respond.

- **Just write.** Stream of consciousness, whatever comes out of your mind. Fill the pages. Any writing process involves reducing quantity to quality.

- **Always have your antenna twitching.** Be receptive to conversations; your own and other people's. It may look strange to someone if you take notes of interesting things they say, but it's better than forgetting them, which you nearly always will.

- **Your own life.** Your experiences are a mine of story ideas, as long as you place them in a dramatic framework and don't expect anyone to be interested in them simply because they're true. As William Goldman wrote, 'Avoid reality.' Reality is mostly uneventful and does not conform to the rules of narrative.

- **Other people's lives.** Look for individual quirks or traits in people you meet. Model a character on a friend (or enemy) or combine elements of several people into one. In chapter 11, Charlie Harris says "A writer should consider himself a student of people," and he's right.

- **Invent a character from the soles of the feet up.** This is best brainstormed by a group - in my screenwriting workshop I'm indebted to Syd Field for the 'Creating A Character' chapter in his book *Screenplay*. His exercise involves creating a character from scratch in as much painstaking detail as possible, thinking carefully about the ramifications of each factor: place, age, period, parents, siblings, sexuality, class, politics, education, job etc. Whenever I do this two-hour exercise with students, I marvel that when you invent a character, you cannot fail to also invent a storyline for them.

- **Invent two skeleton characters, known only by profession.** Give each a singular trait, then give them a reason for meeting, a place for them to meet and an incident to set up or respond to. In other words, something happens to someone, somewhere. You now have a scene, to which you can connect other scenes and other characters.

- **Scan news items on TV/radio and articles in newspapers/magazines.** Truth is often stranger than fiction, so jot down things that intrigue you and rework them later, or try to incorporate them into other scenarios. Cut out items and keep them in a file, but include a few notes of your first impressions to recapture your interest later. Focus on the universality of these ideas - the essence of their emotional appeal to an audience - because alone they won't amount to much, and if they're too personal to you they may not connect with others. Alan Ball's afterword to his *American Beauty* screenplay perfectly illustrates this point: 'I think the idea... first started rattling around in my head during the whole Amy Fisher/Joey Buttafuoco drama [a tragic case in which a young girl shot her married lover's wife]... it struck me: we would never know what really happened. The media circus had already begun, and the story was swiftly being reduced to its most lurid elements, with a cast of cardboard stock characters acting on their basest impulses. But underneath it all were real human lives that had gone horribly astray... That realisation - and an encounter with a plastic bag outside the World Trade Centre - was the basis for what would eventually become *American Beauty*.'

- **Relax.** Close your eyes. Clear your mind and let your imagination drift, without external stimulus or pressure to create. After about an hour, make notes of the images, sounds and feelings you experienced (in that order), and use them as potential jumping-off points. They may be very strange and make little sense, but they do reveal some of your deepest concerns.

- **Dreams.** Again, don't expect logic or linearity, but do use their excess. Dreams are wonderful for conjuring juxtapositions - two or more incongruous elements placed in a surreal connection. Some of my best dreams have included such startling imagery that I've been unable to forget them. Nightmares are better still - what frightens you is likely to frighten others. And, yes, always write them down. Watch David Lynch's films, particularly *Mulholland Drive*, to see dream/nightmare state ingeniously realised on screen.

- **Adapt, or 'borrow.'** If you have a favourite novel or play to which you think you could add something, contact the publisher and enquire about the rights. They may be easier and cheaper to secure than you think. Do not adapt as an academic exercise, you'll only make it worse (example: Scorsese's histrionic remake of the excellent *Cape Fear*). Alternatively, rework or update popular works in the public domain - *Clueless* is Jane Austen's *Emma*, *Cruel Intentions* is Choderlos De Laclos' *Les Liaisons Dangereuses*, both updated to contemporary USA.

Capturing Ideas

Always have an ideas pad near you. Keep one by the phone, by the bed, in your study and on your person wherever you go. If something stimulates you; a phone conversation, an overheard anecdote, mental meanderings on a train journey, a news item, an insight into something you're working on - whatever, wherever, whenever - always write it down.

Our best ideas often hit us when we're least able to process them; at the point of sleep. The discipline is to shake yourself awake, flick on the bedside lamp, take an ideas pad and (working) pen from the bedside table and quickly capture the idea and its flavour, i.e. what you love about it. One night recently I woke at 3 am, electrified by an idea. An hour later it was safely captured and expanded, on paper. Unusually, I was able to form it into a beginning, middle and end, but only because I dealt with it immediately and made the connections. I know these ideas can appear so vital that you think they'll still be accessible in the morning, but trust me, they won't. It's crucial to capture their flavour; if you don't, when you next read them you'll have lost that important rush of excitement you felt at the time.

Writer/director Pedro Almodóvar says: "For me, the first sequence is the key. It's what gives me the drive... It always happens to me. The first sequence I write grabs my interest. I start asking questions about the characters and then I know I have a story to tell. So that first sequence becomes the core of the film, then I develop the story backwards and forwards."

Ideas & Marketing

The time to identify a market for your ideas is way back at the beginning - if you can't, then neither will others. That said, you should still ask yourself a couple of crucial questions about your central premise:

1. Does it have a realistic chance of selling? If the answer's yes, then:

2. Am I sufficiently in love with it to put my heart and soul into it for six to nine months of my life? If the answer's yes again, then do it; if no, then find something else. If the answer to Q1 is no, Q2 remains the same. Your idea might seem completely uncommercial but if it makes you do cartwheels, then stay with it. If your idea has commercial legs but leaves you cold, your script will be luke-warm at best. You have to be fired up about it to make it hot.

If you want to write character-based, dialogue-driven intimate drama, you should be aware that it is unlikely to sell to the feature film market. If you want to write big-budget, widescreen, fast-moving action thrillers, then your work probably won't interest the TV market. Part of marketing involves building knowledge about the requirements of the industry. Reading this book forms one small part of that process.

3. Research & Development

"Maybe it is worth investigating the unknown, if only because the very feeling of not knowing is a painful one."

Krzysztof Kieslowski (Screenwriter/Director)

Research Never Stops

Novice writers often make the fatal mistake of neglecting research. It's not only about authenticity (e.g. learning the minutiae of criminal investigation pro-cedure for a police thriller, or comprehensive details of Victorian London for a story about Jack the Ripper). It also means learning about the film industry and the market place; the great food chain in which you will be competing with thou-sands of others for scraps. Research is the pursuit of any knowledge that will help you keep up with, or get ahead of, the game - and it never stops.

A significant percentage of students arriving at my screenwriting class con-fess to almost never visiting the cinema, or never reading scripts, books or maga-zines about the film industry. It is vital to build an understanding of the industry and the ways in which it operates, and cultivate an informed opinion on what you think works or doesn't work about each film you see and each script you read. You wouldn't apply for a job in an industry you have no knowledge of, so don't expect to write a good script without thoroughly researching the industry and the market, and developing an objective ability to sift diamonds from manure. The more aware you are of the rules the better your chance of success, whether you use them as a template or a point of departure. When you take your first step toward writing a spec screenplay, you become a self-employed manufacturer. If you don't quickly learn to think like one, your product will never sell.

R & D - the more thorough your research, the greater your development.

Know Your Market

If you intend to write for film or television, immerse yourself in those media. Watch plenty of films and programmes, but in an analytical capacity. You are no longer a consumer of moving images. Your desire to write scripts propels you from passivity to activity, and you must comfortably exist on an active plane. Expose yourself to a variety of material that reflects the diversity of today's market place. The wider the range of films/programmes you normally watch, the less work you will have to do. If you only like horror or Westerns or soaps or police dramas, your myopia will cost you. Familiarise yourself with products of different genres and analyse what makes them tick. This common sense imperative often fazes people, perhaps because they aren't used to the concept of personal study outside of academic environments. It's something you need to do if you have a serious ambition to sell your work.

How will you know whether your script stands a chance if you have no knowledge of the market or its demands? How will you know what to include or to avoid in your script? Or to whom it should be sent and how? Or how it should be formatted? Or what font to use? There are hundreds of elements you need to get right when courting the industry. Sending out an unfinished script containing mistakes of structure, layout and presentation, including typographical and grammatical errors, immediately flags you as unprofessional. Even if you later correct these mistakes, you may find it much harder to progress because of the damage your first efforts have caused.

Research Tools

Media products are everywhere; we're bombarded by them on a daily basis. Accessing the means for your research is not difficult. The following list contains the major products and activities you should pursue to maximise your knowledge, and therefore your chances (see the References & Notes chapter for further details).

- **Films/TV programmes**: Watch and analyse, as many as possible. Concentrate on what you like and dislike; what elements work for you or don't, and always try to explain why. If you like it, exactly what was it that you liked? If you didn't, how would you do it differently? Treat this as a self-study programme. Narrow your focus to specific areas like character, dialogue, structure etc.

- **Videos/DVDs**: As above. Many DVDs contain valuable extras including behind-the-scenes documentaries, screenplays, commentaries, internet links etc.

- **Screenwriting literature** - read a selection of these books! They are vitally important in achieving a comprehensive understanding of the medium. I highly recommend titles by Syd Field, Raymond G Frensham, Robert McKee, Ken Dancyger & Jeff Rush, Michael Hauge and Elliot Grove.

- **Film books**: There are many excellent books about the film industry which will build your background knowledge and entertain you at the same time.
- **Trade magazines**: In the UK: *Screen International* (film, weekly); *Broadcast* (TV, weekly). In the US: *Variety* (film, weekly); *Hollywood Reporter* (film/TV, daily).
- **Screenwriting magazines**: Including *Creative Screenwriting*, *Scr(i)pt*, *Scenario* (all US); *Scriptwriter* (UK).
- **Film and related magazines**: Including *Empire*, *Sight & Sound*, *Total Film*, *Uncut*, *Hot Dog*.
- **Broadsheet newspapers**: For daily film/TV news and reviews.
- **Tabloid newspapers**: For daily film/TV scurrilous gossip.
- **Scripts**: In book form (usually transcripts of the finished film) or better still, from the Internet. Go to www.script-o-rama.com for screenplays in various stages from first drafts to shooting scripts.
- **Internet**: The www is the best place to look for all things screen-related. There are legions of sites packed with information on the film and TV business: new releases; old classics; screenwriting; software; production companies; professional and amateur organisations; funding bodies; competitions... the list is endless.
- **Writers groups**: Joining a writers group is an obvious way of sharing the lonely burden of writing. An atmosphere of encouragement and mutual support, coupled with invaluable feedback on problem solving and quality is an ideal nurturing environment for writers.
- **Screenwriting courses/workshops/script reading services**: As London-centric as you'd expect, but beginning to multiply elsewhere - my courses at the University Of Warwick are now in their fifth year. Subscribe to the daily Shooting People newsletter (email writers@shootingpeople.org.uk) for regular adverts and postings, valuable contacts and less valuable debates.
- **University Courses**: Still very few specialist postgraduate courses in the UK, mainly in writing for TV.

The Language Barrier

You should make every effort to learn the complexities of language. Words are the tools of your trade, so if you're unsure about grammar, punctuation and sentence construction, or can't differentiate between nouns, adjectives and verbs, some research is essential. The moving image has also developed its own 'language' over the past century and you should study it to understand how to 'read' images and how to create and communicate meaning using the medium of film.

Development

> "Working and developing and making the script better and better and better, that's the most important thing. If you don't have a good script you don't have anything."

Alan Parker (Director/Screenwriter)

Developing Your Research

Research never stops because knowledge equals power. Thoroughness is the key. Always designate time for research alongside your other activities. Visit libraries, interview people, unearth new contacts or information. If you don't learn, you won't earn.

Developing Your Ideas

OK. Let's assume you've found a concept you like and a promising scenario to build around it. You now want to develop it, but what's the next step? My advice - find out about character and structure. Read chapters 6 and 7 now. Ideas are much easier to develop when they can be situated within a framework, and as you'll see, characters' actions are at the very heart of structure. Then, go back to your idea and arrive at your premise.

Premise

The premise describes what your script is about; the idea or concept at the heart of your story. Try to summarise it in as few words as possible, to tighten your grip on the central concept and memorise it for 'pitching' to interested parties.

Form your premise as a question followed by a complication:

- What happens when a frail old man needs to travel 500 miles to visit his seriously ill brother - but his only mode of transport is a tractor-mower? (*The Straight Story*)

- What happens when a Cockney hardman pursues his daughter's killers in LA - and enters the lion's den with absolutely no fear for his own life? (*The Limey*)

- What happens when a music writer is commissioned by *Rolling Stone* magazine to go on tour with a famous rock band - but he is only 15 years old? (*Almost Famous*)

- What happens when a psychologist treats a young boy who claims to see dead people - but doesn't realise that he too is dead? (*The Sixth Sense*)

Readers situate themselves in your Protagonist's shoes. The premise for *The Sixth Sense* really asks readers to ponder: "What would happen if *I* didn't know I was dead?" This is why you should relate your premise to the problems/tasks facing your hero. The premise of *The Insider* might be: What happens when a conscientious scientist is forced to choose between exposing corporate corruption and protecting himself and his family? However, this excludes chief protagonist Lowell Bergman, so would be better as: What happens when a TV reporter exposes deadly corruption in the tobacco industry, but his actions place his own job and organisation in jeopardy, and his vital inside informant's life and family in danger?

High Concept & Low Concept

The term 'high concept' now defaults to mean plot-driven, fast-moving action films, but in practice refers to any film with a strong, clear, easily-summarised concept that will find an audience on the strength of its premise alone. The assumption within the industry is, the higher the concept, the easier it is to market:

- If James Bond were married, what would he tell his wife he does for a living? (*True Lies*)

- What if living dinosaurs could be created from fossil DNA? (*Jurassic Park*)

- Would you sleep with Robert Redford for $1million? (*Indecent Proposal*)

- What if you could live inside John Malkovich's head? (*Being John Malkovich*)

Some titles are their own premise: *Shakespeare In Love*, *Bad Lieutenant*, *Mars Attacks!*

Low, or soft, concept films tend to have more character-oriented premises which, as Charlie Harris says, rely more on the quality of the end product to attract an audience, and are therefore more risky to potential financiers. Hollywood studio product leans towards high concept, most British and European product towards low concept. Bear this in mind when targeting your market. Write genres for the US and characters for the UK. It's pointless to try to market megabudget science fiction scripts in the UK; ditto political dramas raising awkward questions about American foreign policy in the US (unless set in the US, with a pro-US twist. A fascinating example is Rod Lurie's *Deterrence* - What happens when the US President-elect, snowbound in a Colorado diner when Iraq re-invades Kuwait, threatens a nuclear strike on Baghdad and then has his bluff called?) Remember though that all good scripts contain elements of high and low concept; action and characters combine in a unified premise that addresses and satisfies a wide audience.

Pre-writing

The business of film-making progresses through three stages: pre-production (everything that happens before a foot of film is exposed); production (the film shoot); and post-production (editing, audio dubbing, visual effects, music, captioning etc.). Screenwriting also has three stages: pre-draft, draft and redraft. Drafts and redrafts are covered in chapter 9, so let's look at pre-draft:

Once you've chosen your idea and formed your premise, you'll find yourself making copious notes at any hour of day or night. This is the pre-writing stage when your mind works overtime to produce and keep track of a million disparate, nebulous ideas: images, words, characters, relationships, traits, incidents, locations, plots, sub-plots, emotions, themes and styles. If the premise excites you, you'll be enthusiastic and committed, and think of little else. If it doesn't, you'll do anything to avoid writing.

You need to make clear and comprehensive notes because your brain can't cope with the rush of information. These notes are the missing link between ideas and first draft. They will begin coalescing into something that may, with effort and luck, take on dramatic form and substance. Your notes will steadily connect the disparate elements, piece by slow piece. The picture will form; first in black and white, then colour; first in two dimensions, then three. This is the miracle of creation; the genesis of an organism which did not exist before. Once it does exist, capture the story in a one-page synopsis, including all the major events in chronological sequence (see chapter 8). This will change as your work acquires more depth, and later you'll write a treatment of your plot, but for now use the synopsis as a tool to organise your ideas and keep track of the story.

Ask yourself a few questions about your story: What type of story is it? How does it relate to existing types? What are the recognised story types? For the answers, it's time to learn about Genre.

4. Genre

"Genre is more than formula. More often it is a type of story that has a visceral appeal to its audience. The scriptwriter who ignores the strength of that appeal does so at considerable cost."

Ken Dancyger & Jeff Rush (Screenwriting Lecturers)

The Importance Of Genre

Genre is a French word that means 'type.' Most people are aware of different broad types of films or television programmes. Genre is a shorthand method of categorisation; a buying device that viewers use, consciously or unconsciously, to help them exercise choice over the kind of films or programmes they watch. It is also a selling device for studios and production companies who tend to remain within genre parameters and make the kind of products that have proven popular in the past. Of course, like investments, past performance is no guarantee of future success, but producers wielding multimillion dollar budgets want to give their products the best possible chance of returning a healthy profit for investors (and give themselves the best possible chance of working again).

As you'll see though, genre has significance beyond its use as an easy branding tool. As Dancyger & Rush point out, 'Facts are not as important in genres as dreams... genres are dreamscapes for their audience.'

Familiar Genres

Thriller - Action (*James Bond, Enemy Of The State, Die Hard*)

Thriller - Adventure (*Raiders Of The Lost Ark, The Mummy, The Mask Of Zorro*)

Thriller - Psychological (*Fight Club, Silence Of The Lambs, Seven*)

Thriller - Crime (*Heat, LA Confidential, The Long Good Friday*)

Science Fiction (*2001: A Space Odyssey, The Matrix, Alien*)

Western (*Unforgiven, Dances With Wolves, The Searchers*)

War (*Saving Private Ryan, Full Metal Jacket, Apocalypse Now*)

Epic (*Gladiator, Braveheart, Spartacus*)

Horror (*The Blair Witch Project, Halloween, Night Of The Living Dead*)

Comedy (*A Fish Called Wanda, Life Of Brian, Airplane*)

Black Comedy (*Happiness, Your Friends & Neighbors, The War Of The Roses*)

Romantic Comedy (*Bridget Jones' Diary, The Wedding Singer, Notting Hill*)

Romantic Drama (*Sleepless In Seattle, The Bridges Of Madison County, Captain Corelli's Mandolin*)

Period Drama (*The Remains Of The Day, La Veuve De Saint Pierre, Elizabeth*)

Social Drama (*My Name Is Joe, Nil By Mouth, American History X*)

Biographical Drama (*Gods And Monsters, Shadowlands, Amadeus*)

Musical Drama (*Moulin Rouge, West Side Story, The Sound Of Music*)

Adult/Erotic Drama (*In The Realm Of The Senses, Intimacy, Eyes Wide Shut*)

Fantasy (*Lord Of The Rings, Conan The Barbarian, Time Bandits*)

Art Narrative (*Eraserhead, L'Avventura, Koyaanisqatsi*)

Animation (*A Bug's Life, The Iron Giant, The Nightmare Before Christmas*)

Documentary (*When We Were Kings, One Day In September, The Thin Blue Line*)

Television genres include: Quiz Show, Soap Opera, Documentary (much more common to television than to film), Animation (ditto), Current Affairs, Chat Show (Talk Show in the US), Game Show, Situation Comedy, Police or Detective Drama, Docusoap (documentary meets soap opera, featuring the lives/occupations of 'real' people), 'Reality TV' (the *Big Brother*-led phenomenon of the docusoap taken to its extreme, featuring 'real' people living together in an artificially created environment), plus many of the film genres listed above.

Genre Evolution

Genres do not stand still. They are in constant flux and their boundaries widen as writers and film-makers seek to add new dimensions. Consider the oldest of all genres, the Western: traditionally infused with the American self-image of pioneering spirit, triumph over the adversary (hostile Indians), triumph over adversity (inhospitable landscape), building the new frontier, bringing order to chaos, civilisation to the wilderness and law to the lawless, it mutated as different interpretations of the period and place emerged. Sam Peckinpah (*The Wild Bunch*) and the Italian Spaghetti Westerns of Sergio Leone and others in the 1960s/early 1970s reinvented the genre as a battleground of the seven deadly sins and introduced a new strain of cynicism, black humour and violence. Later, films like *Dances With Wolves* and *Unforgiven* posed uncomfortable questions about the Western myth: was not the triumph over 'hostile Indians' in actuality the subjugation and genocide of a people whose only crime was that they were there first? Was the common man not forced to commit acts of savagery to simply survive among the jackals, in some cases with sickening relish? We can see the progression of the genre from rose-tinted heroism through savage realism to social conscience.

Genres do not exist in isolation, but always in relation to others. There are also subgenres which further complicate matters; for example Comedy encompasses Black Comedy (with a darker, often unsettling tone), Romantic Comedy (comedy of relationships), Period Comedy (often comedy of manners), Farce (a particularly British humour), Screwball (a particularly American humour), Satire (often ridiculing social structures), Parody (often ridiculing other genres) and so on. Genres can also form hybrids with other genres. For example, as well as Comedy we can have Comedy Science Fiction (*Spaceballs*, *Red Dwarf*), Comedy Western (*Blazing Saddles*), Black Comedy Fantasy (*Brazil*) and so on.

Conventions & Motifs

Each genre contains its own conventions and motifs. Conventions are the way things are usually done; in the Western good guys usually win, bad guys wear black, there's a final showdown, the Protagonist's motive is based on revenge or imposing law and order etc. Motifs are recurring elements which the audience expects to see. Western motifs include cowboys, Indians, horses, wagon trains, small wooden shanty towns with saloons, livery stables, a jailhouse, six-guns and rifles. Science fiction motifs include spaceships, faster-than-light travel, aliens, silver bodysuits, laser guns.

TV soap opera conventions include a community with a hub or meeting place like a bar or coffee shop; storylines focusing on tensions within families or the community; births, deaths and marriages; characters leaving; new characters arriving; a cliffhanger ending to seduce viewers to tune in next time to find out what happens etc.

Using Genre

It could be argued that film narrative is itself a form of genre, as it relies on structure, conventions and familiarity. If you want to write commercial film scripts, you'll need a working knowledge of genre to utilise or, better still, transcend the conventions of the genres you write in. Locate your ideas within a generic framework as well as a structural one, and have fun either using genre conventions, updating them or intelligently subverting them. Analyse films which cross-pollinate genres against the grain - incorporating incongruous elements normally associated with unrelated genres, to offer something unfamiliar.

The relocation of the big city cop thriller to the rolling fields of the Amish community in *Witness*, combined with many elements of the romance genre, is a master stroke of playing with genre conventions. The Coen brothers often create memorable characters against genre: think of 'Mad Max' biker Leonard Smalls in *Raising Arizona*; schizophrenic psychopath Charlie Meadows/Karl Mundt in *Barton Fink*; or laid-back pregnant sheriff Marge Gundersen in *Fargo*.

Some films begin in one genre and end in another - *From Dusk Till Dawn* flips from crime to horror without warning. Steve DeJarnatt's *Miracle Mile* masterfully segues from romantic drama to Armageddon via the best screen telephone call ever. Hitchcock's *Vertigo* begins as a romantic melodrama with supernatural overtones, before debunking the supernatural (almost slapping our wrists for being taken in) then burrowing uncomfortably deep into the Protagonist's mental illness.

David Lynch has made a career out of subverting genre conventions; in *Lost Highway* he goes as far as changing his Protagonist into a completely different character halfway through (and includes the second-best screen telephone call ever).

Exercise: The next few times you go to the cinema or watch a film on TV or video, write down what genre(s) you think the film belongs to, and the conventions/motifs you recognise. Try to come up with ways in which they could be extended or challenged.

Five Genre-Defining Movies

2001: A Space Odyssey (science fiction [as opposed to 'Hollywood' science fiction]); *Night Of The Living Dead* (horror); *The Godfather I & II* (gangster); *Lawrence Of Arabia* (epic); *Love Story* (romance).

5. Story & Plot

"Steven Spielberg and George Lucas have changed the way stories are told for the first time since Homer. They're told now like amusement park rides."

John Milius (Director/Screenwriter)

"...even the most advanced robot tells a lousy story."

Lew Hunter (Screenwriting Lecturer)

Understanding Story & Plot

To understand the function of story and plot, it is important to distinguish between them. Many people refer to one when they mean the other. The difference is simple, but crucial:

Story - all of the elements contained within the narrative, in chronological order. In other words, everything that happens to all of the characters placed in a straight line through time.

Plot - how the writer chooses to order the story elements; intercutting main plots and sub-plots, and incorporating flashbacks, flashforwards etc. if necessary.

Story, Character, Incident, Structure

After our genre digression, let's get straight back to your story. Your premise is exciting and your notes are progressing at a furious rate. At this stage you'll be thinking in story terms - beginning, middle, end - when developing your material, but the problem of how to organise the plot will constantly nag at the back of your mind. Keep it there for now. Only begin plotting when you have all of your main story events and you're ready to sequence them.

Don't be tempted to construct your events too skeletally and neglect the key ingredients of your story - characters and incidents. The narrative world can't exist without them, they are inextricably intertwined. If you treat the story development as an academic exercise, even in a whodunnit mystery, your work will be sterile and airless, and your characters won't be able to breathe. The mechanics of cause and effect are always secondary to inventing and communicating a living world with a consistent set of rules. The world of your story should feel as realistic to readers as their own, and your characters must be equally realistic to live there.

STORY is formed by characters' actions as they cause or react to incidents, overcome obstacles and pursue goals.

CHARACTERS cannot act without goals to strive for, problems to overcome and incidents to respond to.

INCIDENTS need to be seen from the perspective of their effects on characters' lives, to give readers a human element with which to identify.

STRUCTURE is the framework which supports the story and supplies the most drama, conflict and tension to draw readers in and maintain their emotional involvement.

The story world (macrocosm) must be presented through characters and incidents (microcosm). Even in a large-scale genre thriller like *Heat*, the cops-and-robbers macrocosm is boiled down to the Vincent Hanna versus Neil McCauley microcosm. The bravura daylight set pieces would have far less impact without examining each character's specific behavioural attitudes to them before, during and after.

Theme

When pitching your project to someone important, don't be surprised if, after you tell them the premise, they say "Okay - but what's it *really* about?" What they're asking for is the theme. They're also asking whether or not *you* know it. If you don't, there's an old Hollywood maxim that goes "If your script is about what it's about, you're in deep shit."

Your script must be about more than it appears to be on the surface. Not only in terms of plot and sub-plot, but also theme. The theme is the expression of the universal value of your story; the reason why it will connect with an audience. It may not arrive in your mind until your script is finished, but it will spring from what motivated you to write your script in the first place. What they are actually asking you is "What do you really want to *say*?" Theme can be expressed in one word (revenge, integrity, greed, justice), but this doesn't tell anyone much. Something like "The amazing ability of the human spirit to triumph over adversity, or against the odds" is better, but you'll be politely told that most stories fit this description. Try to be specific about your particular theme.

Themes are about emotion. Your primary task as a screenwriter is to convey the emotional impact of your script to a reader. This is one difference between a cinematic and a televisual premise. The cinematic premise may be action or character-oriented, but should connect and resonate with the audience's emotions on a level that a televisual premise cannot. It's not just about exaggeration, it's also about sustaining an emotionally charged narrative for two hours and keeping an audience engaged. After being shot, Andy Warhol said "People sometimes say that the way things happen in the movies is unreal. But actually it's the way things happen to you in life that's unreal. The movies make emotions look so strong and real, whereas when things really do happen to you, it's like watching television. You don't feel anything."

In a great script there may be several themes. One in *Field Of Dreams* is Second Chances: If you were granted another chance to have something that you only realised was important when it was gone, how far would you go to take it? To Ray Frensham, the theme is: "It is important for us to have dreams - even if those dreams are not ultimately fulfilled, it is important for us to have them." Many themes are present because of the skilful layering and essential humanity in Phil Alden Robinson's script.

Conflict & Tension

Syd Field says, "Without conflict there is no drama." Conflict arises from situation, but more importantly from character, and should be present in every scene. The goals and needs of the Protagonist meet opposition from without (other characters or situations) and from within (inner demons, conscience, fear, ghosts), creating conflict. Tension builds in the gaps between eruptions of conflict, but is also ever-present in the opposing goals or values of characters. Every major character needs polarities, within themselves and in their relationship to others. Polarities create conflict and tension. Include some form of conflict in every scene: physical, psychological, situational. When you lose sight of conflict, you also lose readers' interest.

Building & Releasing Tension

The opening sequence of Robert Harmon's horror thriller, *The Hitcher*: A young man (C Thomas Howell), exhausted from driving in the rain all night, picks up a soaking hitch-hiker (Rutger Hauer) in the middle of nowhere. The young man then runs an incredibly tense gauntlet as the hitch-hiker first refuses to say where he's headed, then sticks a knife in his face and relates in graphic detail how he cut up the last guy who gave him a ride, and tells him he's to meet the same fate unless he can stop him. Finally the young man summons the courage and strength to lunge at the hitch-hiker - who falls out of the door he left ajar. The young man yells and slams the dash in a frenzy of freed tension as the hitch-hiker bounces along the dark, wet road. CUT TO:

INT/EXT. Desert Road - Day. The young man is taking it easy. A station wagon overtakes. Two children in the rear window pretend to shoot him with toy guns. Smiling, he 'shoots' back with his finger, then freezes as slowly, between the two children, arms around their shoulders, rises the hitch-hiker... A textbook lesson on the rhythms of tension. Slowly build to a crescendo, then release... and immediately start to build again.

Reversing Expectation

You're watching a film. You're thinking "I know what's going to happen next." You experience a slight rush of anticipation. Then, it happens. Exactly as you thought. And you feel... disappointed. The slight rush was because you secretly hoped that it *wouldn't* happen; that the film would surprise you, show you something clever and unexpected. I remember watching *Fatal Attraction*, sitting behind two old ladies who kept whispering to each other what they thought would happen next. Normally this would incur my wrath, but this time I kept quiet and listened - and they were right, every time, because they found the film's reversals and switches so predictable. Try to subvert expectations of genre as well as story.

When developing your story, ask yourself what you would expect to happen next if this were someone else's script - and then don't do it. Reverse it. As often as possible. If you can place a few major and several minor reversals in your script, that readers won't see coming, then you'll keep them turning the pages. It's about uncertainty, and the building of suspense. If you also reverse the tone, then even better. A few memorable reversals:

- In *Quiz Show*, we expect Goodwin to dismiss Herb Stempel's allegations against Van Doren and walk away, which he does - until Herb desperately confesses that he was also given the questions in advance.

- In *Leon*, during Matilda's rifle lesson, we think *surely* Leon won't let her just shoot the jogger in Central Park.

- In *Diva*, we think Jules is doomed as Le Curé stands over him with a knife until Gorodish appears out of thin air to spray knockout gas in his face.

- The final scenes of *Get Carter* and *The Long Good Friday* are so powerful because the best reversals are kept until the end.

Raiders Of The Lost Ark has several neat reversals: Toht's ominous-looking instrument of torture which turns out to be a folding coat hanger; Indy calmly pulling his gun to shoot the huge swordsman after defeating countless other thugs using only his whip; Indy leaving Marion bound and gagged in the tent rather than raise the alarm by rescuing her.

Ellipsis

Simply, cutting out the dead time. Real life consists of millions of dull moments interspersed with a few vital, dramatic ones - if you could tune in to Tom Cruise's life for days on end, you would be mostly bored to tears. Story world and real world are in fact worlds apart. In *The Truman Show*, Truman Burbank's every waking hour is manipulated in an artificial environment for a unique TV show. Once he becomes aware of this, he has to escape the cloying story world and gain his freedom. Similarly, in *EdTV*, the TV execs realise that Ed's life just isn't interesting enough to the viewers without dramatic intervention. Screenwriting excises the boring 'real world' moments and gives characters a series of vital, dramatic situations compressed into a narrative framework. Ellipsis allows these events to appear connected and seamless, almost as though they were playing out in real time.

Screen Time & Narrative Time

Screen time is the duration of the film; usually 1½ - 2 hours, based on the average audience's attention span. Narrative time is the duration of the story events. This can be real time (*High Noon*'s narrative clock begins ticking at 10:30 am; the showdown is at, er, noon), decades (in *Back To The Future* and *Pleasantville*, the protagonists are displaced from the present to the 1950s), or several millennia (*2001: A Space Odyssey* moves from the Dawn of Man to a space mission to Jupiter). A tip: if you're writing for a low-budget independent market, compress your script's narrative time into weeks rather than months, days rather than weeks. Try not to include exterior locations showing seasonal changes - it's too expensive.

Start At The End

The earlier you know your climax/finale/dénouement, the easier the writing process becomes. If you are secure in the knowledge that you have a satisfying resolution, your confidence will be greater. On a more practical level, you can write 'backwards,' setting in place everything that narrows focus to your climax, rather than writing reams of exploratory material in the hope that it will lead to a tight and exciting conclusion.

Great Scenes

When the memory of a film has faded into a blur, the great scenes are the ones people remember. You'll be able to recall dozens of your own favourites without too much thought. Every script should contain a handful of scenes that provide memorable, standout moments where the reader thinks "Wow, I wish I'd written that!" If one of your script's great moments is its climax, you're ahead of the game. You'll know them by the time you come to write the first draft. They'll be the scenes that set your pulse racing; exciting, vital, inspired and almost fully-formed in your mind's eye. You're itching to see them in the movie and you can visualise them down to the smallest detail.

In *The Double Life Of Véronique* there are four beautiful set piece scenes: in the square during the demonstration when Veronika tries to collect her spilled sheet music, then watches in awe as her identical double is herded back on board a French tour coach; Veronika's tragic concert début; the poignant puppet show at the junior school where Véronique teaches music; the café meeting when the puppet master reveals the devastating reason why he has been sending her 'clues' to bring her to this place at this time.

Plot

"Your characters... are the vehicles through which the audience experiences emotion, like the cars on the roller coaster. The plot structure involves the events of the story and the way they are positioned and is like the curves and turns of the track on the ride. The layout of the track will determine whether or not the ride is exciting."

Michael Hauge (Screenwriting Lecturer)

Cut & Paste

Once your major story events are laid out in chronological form, you can move on to the complexities of plotting. As Jean-Luc Godard said, "A film should have a beginning, a middle and an end, but not necessarily in that order."

Plots may or may not follow a linear progression. In *Pulp Fiction*, the first story event occurs when the young Butch is given his dead father's gold watch by one of his army colleagues, but this event is placed an hour into the plot. *Citizen Kane* opens with the death of Charles Foster Kane, and the plot then flashes backwards and forwards, piecing together a jigsaw of Kane's character by relating key events from his life as witnessed by those closest to him. In *Memento*, the narrative again begins with the last story event, then runs backwards in short overlapping segments, the plot structure cleverly paralleling the protagonist Leonard's ten-minute memory span. *The Limey* is a patchwork quilt of fleeting non-sequential images layered together to form a complex emotional mood.

Before you order your plot events, you should have five fixed points established in your mind: opening sequence, climax/resolution, two end of act watershed incidents (plot points) and your mid-point. The art of plotting revolves around trying to find the most effective dramatic structure for your story. See chapter 6 for ways in which plot and structure intertwine.

Main Plot

The main plot follows the protagonist's action line through the story. It connects with his outer motivations and the obstacles he faces. The main plot forms the immediate foreground of the narrative and carries the major thrust: to get the hero from the inciting incident to his goal in around one hundred pages.

Sub-Plots

Sub-plots involve other characters and events that connect directly or indirectly to the protagonist's main plot. The foremost sub-plot reveals the protagonist's inner struggle to conquer those elements within himself that stand in his way. Other characters and events may be connected to each other, but they are all somehow connected to the protagonist and his actions. They may run parallel to the main plot, or counter to it. Cutting to sub-plots is a way to create anticipation in the reader by delaying the resolution of elements or tensions in the main plot. Sub-plots are also useful carriers of theme. The protagonist's main plot is usually concerned with his actions to solve problems, complete tasks or achieve goals, but the theme that resonates with an audience may concern a sub-plot involving romance or injustice or hardship or anything that conveys the true emotion of your story.

Exposition

The reader needs to be provided with information about the context of your script; the background to the events of the plot. In a science fiction story set in the future or on a distant planet, you will need to inform the reader how the world evolved from the world we're familiar with, or what particular conditions exist in this alien environment. Obviously you don't have time or space to supply a full future history, but you must supply the information relevant to the story. This is known as setting your exposition, and applies to characters as well as events. Your characters have lived lives which have brought them to their start point and set up their individual and collective narratives. Events in their recent past will particularly influence who and how they are when readers first encounter them. As Lajos Egri said, "Motivation must have grown out of what happened *before* the story started. Your story is *possible only because it grew out of the very thing that happened before.*" How you choose to relate these significant 'backstories' will require a lot of thought, and may result in shifts along your narrative timeline. Voice-overs, flashbacks, flashforwards etc. are satisfying plot devices when well-crafted, but for a novice screenwriter they present problems of complexity and are often badly executed. The characters cannot tell their own stories; you must show the relevant events and incorporate them into your plot. You must also do this quickly; readers need to know what's going on and why, as soon as it happens. Most if not all of your expository detail should be placed in Act I, to set up the complications that occur in Act II.

That said, holding back a crucial element of exposition can maximise readers' anticipation. In *Jaws*, a Great White shark is cruising around Amity Island, killing swimmers and ruining the tourist trade. Three disparate individuals join forces to hunt it. Chief Brody has a big city background and doesn't even like water. Hooper is an ambitious but unproven marine biologist. Boat Captain Quint is an enigma because his backstory is deliberately delayed. He's driven, abrasive and opinionated, but his past is an unknown quantity. He is the focus of the tensions between the three men as they hunt the killer shark, and of the crucial 'drinking' scene after the shark first gets away. This memorable scene is multifunctional; it solves the problem of how to bond the men together to function as a unit, and culminates in Quint's superb 'USS Indianapolis' monologue which finally delivers his backstory (worth the wait), establishes his credentials, clarifies his motivation to kill the shark and brings the difficulty of their task into sharp relief.

Exercise: Watch one of your favourite films and write down a brief summary of the major plot events. Place the events in story (i.e. chronological) order. Observe how the main plot and sub-plots are arranged in relation to each other, and time. Write down the relevant events that took place before the film begins, and the characters' backstories. How is this information given? Can you think of other ways the details could have been shown?

Five Great Plots To Study

Pulp Fiction; Citizen Kane; Rashomon; The Double Life Of Véronique; Chinatown

6. Character & Dialogue

"Let's get in character."

Jules Winnfield (Pulp Fiction)

"I am interested in what happens to people when they must adapt to a new world."

Jean Renoir (Screenwriter/Director)

The Puppet Master

At the heart of your script are your characters, and you are God, with the power of life or death over them. It's your choice to make their day or break their bones. You decide whether they: begin a beautiful friendship or end one in tears; do the decent thing or the lowdown dirty one; stand up and be counted or lie down and take what's coming. That's some responsibility. Your duty as a deity is to mould your characters in three dimensions, and project them alive and kicking into readers' minds. If their construction is flawed, it is because your constructive powers are flawed.

Although you are the animator of your creations, it is important that you allow them to exist independently of you; to give them the freedom to grow and develop within your plot. If your characters' traits are all facets of yourself, or if they all speak with your voice, then you will fail to convince readers that they are living, breathing people. It's like parenthood: you bring them into the world, care for them and nurture them, but ultimately your greatest service is preparing them to exist on their own out there among them English.

Giving Characters Life

Characters are rarely presented from birth; usually they have lived for many years before we meet them, and have evolved complex individual personalities. Your job is to burrow as far inside their minds as possible. Write a profile for each character, a resumé of their lives from birth until the opening of the narrative: their parents' social class and circumstances, location and occupation(s), whether they stayed in one place or were frequently uprooted, whether they had a happy, sad or tragic childhood, whether or not they were popular with the opposite sex (or the same sex), whether they left school early or went to university, their political views, whether they married young or had a string of lovers or chose celibacy, whether they embarked on a successful career or drifted through meaningless jobs - all the major forces that have acted upon their personality to form them into the person the reader encounters. As you'll see, this is also a potential short cut to their story.

Your characters must *feel* real. They can be odd as hell, operate on as skewed a logic as you care to invent, but they must be consistent within their own warped reality. Good recent examples of believable, rounded, interesting oddballs include Tracey Flick in *Election*, Max Fisher in *Rushmore*, James Leer in *Wonder Boys* and the strange but mesmerising 'romance' between Enid and Seymour in *Ghost World*.

Protagonist & Antagonist

Two characters have locked horns in the majority of fiction films since the early days of narrative cinema. These are the good guy and the bad guy; properly the Protagonist and the Antagonist, popularly the Hero and the Villain. Most film narratives revolve around the actions of the Hero as he tries to achieve a personal goal and the efforts of the Villain to prevent him from doing so. According to Joseph Campbell there are three classic types of Hero: Dramatic, Tragic, Comic. The Dramatic Hero succeeds due to his best efforts, the Tragic Hero fails despite his best efforts, and the Comic Hero succeeds despite his best efforts. The lot of the classic Villain is ultimately to become a Dead Villain, as long as he has given the Hero the absolute fight of his life.

Example: *Quiz Show*

All screenwriting tenets (except format) are generalisations rather than rules and there are always exceptions. In *Quiz Show*, the role of Protagonist is not clear cut. Dick Goodwin's investigation of the TV quiz shows is the driving force, but Charles Van Doren and Herb Stempel are also given large chunks of screen time. Goodwin wants to make his mark and to be a force for change, in that order. Van Doren is seduced by the power of TV, the lure of fame and fortune and the opportunity to escape from the shadow of his famous father. He moves from hubris to humility when he confesses his deceit in front of his family and the American public. Stempel is also seduced, and when his promised 'career' in TV is revealed as a lie, he takes the only revenge open to him - telling his story. Corporate America is the Antagonist. NBC is placed on trial for its underhand practices but the pawns are left to take the flak while the executives sit above the law in their ivory towers. Paul Attanasio's brilliant script is an object lesson in how to construct a complex portrait of time, place and situation through multilayered and compelling characters.

Goal-Driven Protagonist

The goal-driven Protagonist begins the narrative single-mindedly pursuing a specific set of personal goals, or at least with those wheels set in motion. We know at the outset, or soon after, what he wants, how he intends to get it and the essential problems he faces. The plot is formed by the actions he takes to achieve his goals or perform his tasks.

- In *The Limey*, Cockney ex-con Dave Wilson travels to Los Angeles to discover his daughter's killers and avenge her death.

- In *The Long Good Friday*, Harold Shand is set to seal the backing of an American consortium for his ambitious plan to redevelop London's Docklands.

- In *The Last Seduction*, Bridget Gregory runs off with $700,000 from a drug deal carried out by her unwitting husband Clay.

Passive Protagonist

Alternatively, the Protagonist may begin as a passive character, but he must be quickly forced to become active by events beyond his control. There are two types of passive Protagonist; those who are perfectly at home in their normal world (let's call them 'Insiders') and those who are not at all comfortable in theirs ('Outsiders'). When displaced from the ordinary world into the extraordinary world, both have to figure a new set of rules as they go along, as they (and the reader) discover their limits when placed in extreme situations.

Insiders

Insiders are stable and/or happy when we meet them; they have what they want, and are oblivious to the explosion that's about to blast them out of their normal world and into the 'special' world. We then follow the actions they take to recover their former equilibrium or to explore and make the best of their new set of circumstances.

- In *Trading Places*, Louis Winthorpe III is a smug Ivy League financial whizz-kid whose life explodes as a result of a whimsical bet, when he is framed for theft by his employers and replaced by a homeless street con artist.

- In *House Of Games*, Dr Margaret Ford is a renowned psychiatrist and best-selling author who encounters a world she never imagined when, to aid a suicidal client, she confronts a gangster who threatened to kill him over a gambling debt.

- In *The Edge*, billionaire Chârles Morse's plane crashes in remote, inhospitable terrain. His wealth is useless in his battle against the elements, a killer grizzly and perhaps his wife's lover for survival and a return to his former life.

Outsiders

Outsiders are somehow different from those around them, they just don't fit into their world; classic square pegs in round holes. This sense of being outside their lives can ease their transition to the special world, as they didn't really belong in their own.

- In *American Beauty*, Lester Burnham is deep in mid-life crisis. He dislikes his job, his life and his family, of whose contempt he is all too aware. His problem is loss of self-esteem, but once he decides that it's never too late to get it back, he relentlessly pursues his inner vitality until the worm has turned a full 360 degrees.

- In *The Straight Story*, frail 73-year-old farmer Alvin Straight is a stubborn old curmudgeon in failing health. His major problem arrives when he receives word of his estranged brother's serious illness. He's lost his driver's license because of his eyesight and his restricted mobility, so he embarks on a 500-mile journey across three states - on a motorised lawnmower!

- In *The Terminator*, Sarah Connor is unfulfilled and apathetic, trapped in a dead-end waitressing job and lacking a relationship. When she suddenly finds herself catapulted into a nightmare - hunted by a superhuman cyborg programmed to kill her and thus prevent the birth of her son who will lead humanity's resistance against the machines in a devastating future war - she finds a true purpose and starts living instead of merely existing.

Example: *Made In Heaven*

A memorable Outsider Protagonist is Mike Shea in *Made In Heaven* (cross-reference these examples with the section on Structure in chapter 8).

We open in black & white. Mike is in a cinema with his parents and girl-friend, watching the final few seconds of Hitchcock's *Notorious* (not only does this allow the slyly ironic device of a title card showing 'The End' at the beginning, it also establishes period). His girlfriend whispers "Don't we lead such mundane lives?" Things seem good, but afterwards at dinner the atmosphere becomes tense when she brings up his recent job loss. His father insists his boy was laid off, not fired. Undeterred, she tells Mike to ask old school 'friend' Orin for a job in the bank. Reluctantly he does and, when turned down, tells Orin exactly what he's always thought of him. Soon after, while necking in his battered car, Mike suggests to her that they start a new life in California. She drops the bomb that her boss kind of asked her to marry him... and she kind of said yes!

Each pillar of his life is taken down, one by one: job, relationship, self-esteem. With no reason to stay, he sets out for California with just his dog for company. So far, so promising. But writers Bruce Evans & Raynold Gideon are just warming up. Not long after setting out, he happens upon an accident; a pick-up truck has gone into a river, and children are trapped inside. He dives in and heroically rescues them, but when the pick-up slides under the water his dog is left whining on the bridge as he fails to resurface. Dissolve from black & white to colour as he stands naked in a brightly-lit room and is greeted by his Aunt Lisa. His *dead* Aunt Lisa...

Empathy & Sympathy

As has oft been said, events on the page/screen are a mirror for the reader/ audience to observe themselves. Make your protagonist empathetic by giving them qualities that allow readers maximum involvement in their predicament; to put themselves in their shoes for the duration. They should also be sympathetic. Not an all-round jolly good egg, but a complex, ambiguous character with shades of good and bad; in other words a believable, three-dimensional, flawed but intriguing human being, capable of doing the unexpected. There is more than a suspension of disbelief going on here; your characters are the audience's avatars. If we always know what they'll do, where is the suspense?

Don't confuse sympathy with likeability. Many dislikeable protagonists about whom we feel ambivalent remain unforgettable anti-heroes: Charles Foster Kane is a temperamental megalomaniac; Travis Bickle in *Taxi Driver* is a bitter, burned-out psychopath; Griffin Mill in *The Player* will tread on anyone to safeguard his own position and status; Johnny in *Naked* is a nihilistic egotist who uses his intellect as a weapon; Dennis Hopper as the eponymous *Paris Trout* is a murderer, bigot and wife-torturer. Yet their charisma keeps our interest and their character flaws elicit our sympathy.

It's a fine and subjective line. If your protagonist is a complete bastard with no redeeming qualities he'll be unsympathetic, so your task is to make him truly memorable. If he is whiter than white, or lacking motivation, he'll be boring. If he is a stereotype, he'll be flat and two-dimensional. If he is invincible, the so-what factor kicks in. The danger in each case is that readers will neither root for your Protagonist, nor care what happens to him.

Credibility

If readers do not believe your hero capable of a particular action or of reaching his goal they will suspend their suspension of disbelief and you'll lose their attention. Characters are often pitched into incredible situations, *but they must remain in character to negotiate them*. If your characters perform extraordinary or inexplicable feats that you have failed to set up, readers won't buy it.

In *Kansas City*, the character of Carolyn Stilton, stoned on opium for the entire narrative, suddenly shoots protagonist Blondie O'Hara. This provides an unsatisfactory resolution that rings completely false. There is no foreshadowing to suggest she is capable of doing this. In *Casino*, during the opening flashforward sequence we see De Niro's character blown to smithereens by a car bomb. For emphasis, he floats through a sea of flames in a stylised title sequence. So when the big moment finally arrives and he crawls away from the inferno with only singed pride, it feels like what it is - a big cheat. In *What Lies Beneath*, the characters' actions or choices are constantly baffling, and many character connections are set up only to remain frustratingly unresolved. I'm sure you can pick your own examples.

Hollywood science fiction has consistently lacked credibility and treated its audience as idiots. Since the advent of Lucas & Spielberg, even dying has been reduced to a minor inconvenience (Obi-Wan Kenobi, E.T.). *Superman* (Lois Lane) and the *Star Trek* franchise (Spock) followed suit. Don't get suckered into this for your characters. Watch *Bambi* for the best example of the power of death, *Run Lola Run* and *Vertigo* for ingenious ways to cheat it, and *The Sixth Sense* and *The Others* for fresh and inventive treatments of it.

Fears

You need to know, and show, the thing your character fears most; their worst nightmare made manifest. Leon's fear is change; the spanner in his well-oiled machine of personal control. Griffin Mill's is losing his prestigious position and being convicted of murder. Lester Burnham's is self-stagnation and inertia. Harold Shand's is the failure of his big deal. Charles Morse's is that people only like him because of his wealth; even his wife. Fears provide negative motivation for characters just as goals provide positive ones.

Ghost

The ghost is something in the hero's backstory from which he can't hide. It haunts him. It is the part of himself he must exorcise to overcome his greatest obstacle. It could be a fatal error of judgement, failure to overcome a previous antagonist, his own insecurity or self-hatred. Whatever it is, it must connect with the obstacles faced this time, creating self-doubt and uncertainty.

Alvin Straight's ghosts are his alcohol-fuelled fall-out with his brother, and accidentally shooting a WWII colleague. In a bar near the end of his journey, he tells a stranger this story for the first time and conquers his fear of alcoholism as he takes his first beer in ten years. Dave Wilson's is guilt for spending most of his daughter's life in jail. In *The Crying Game*, Fergus' ghost is that he's responsible for the death of Dil's ex-lover.

40

Plural- & Multiprotagonists

The protagonist need not be a single character. It's quite common to find multiples, from partnerships like Bob Hope and Bing Crosby, Rock Hudson and Doris Day, most 'buddy movies,' to ensemble casts in *The Big Chill*, *Magnolia*, *Grand Canyon* and *Go*. Robert McKee has defined two types of multiple: Plural-Protagonist, where both or all share the same goals and mutually suffer and benefit (*Butch Cassidy And The Sundance Kid*, *Alien*); and Multiprotagonist, where both or all pursue separate, independent goals and desires (*Short Cuts*, *Traffic*, *Pulp Fiction*). The more protagonists you employ, the more you increase the difficulty of your task; you must ensure that both or all are equally three-dimensional, believable, complex, empathetic individuals.

Protagonist & Structure

Character function is synergetic with structure. The rhythms of the plot are formed by the protagonist as he scrambles up ladders or slides down snakes, but (as you'll see in chapter 8) this synergy is forged in a much deeper, complex and intertwining matrix. Whether initially driven or passive, pursuing a new goal (Alvin's crazy journey) or an old life (Louis' quest to clear his name and regain his status), dragged into a fight to the death (Sarah striving first to escape and then defeat the Terminator) or a no-win scenario (Jimmy the Saint's 'choice' between a deadly job or losing his business in *Things To Do In Denver When You're Dead*), the protagonist is the vehicle that carries the reader through the narrative. Whether dramatic, tragic or comic, be sure to make him heroic (even if he's an anti-hero, his major choice should be an heroic one; or if it isn't, therein lies his downfall).

Antagonist

Like most protagonists, most antagonists are wilful, driven characters. The goals of the villain oppose those of the hero and the two will come into direct conflict over this polarity. Memorable villain roles offer actors a delicious opportunity to chew scenery and steal the picture from under the Hero's nose. Who watches Kevin Costner's Robin when Alan Rickman's reptilian Sheriff of Nardingham (sorry, Nottingham) is around in the otherwise forgettable *Robin Hood, Prince Of Thieves*? Who doesn't experience a thrill of horrified fascination at the sheer, er, alienness of the creature in *Alien*, and a secret desire to see it stalk its human prey? Who can take their eyes off Dennis Hopper's definitive psycho Frank Booth in *Blue Velvet*? Who can shake the unforgettable moment when evil Barnes guns down fellow Sergeant Elias in *Platoon*? Memorable antagonists exert a powerfully intoxicating appeal to the bad guy in all of us.

Perhaps the major quality required of an antagonist is that he is in almost every respect at least the equal of the protagonist. This generates maximum tension and propels the narrative right down to the wire. In the archetypal Cops and Robbers conflict, *Heat*, protagonist Vincent Hanna is the SuperCop whose wired dedication to his job is consuming his life and wrecking his third marriage. Antagonist Neil McCauley is the SuperThief whose crew is taking down increasingly mammoth scores and needs just one last one before quitting. Hanna knows McCauley's a real hot dog, and it's imperative that he takes him down. McCauley knows Hanna has rumbled some of the best crews, but will not allow anything to get in his way. Their cat-and-mouse game is played for the highest possible stakes. Each is the very best at what he does and when they come face to face over a coffee like regular guys - volatile, passionate Hanna and ice cool, understated McCauley, Pacino and De Niro - it is electrifying cinema. The protagonist and antagonist should be so closely matched that the outcome is in doubt until the final moments: the Irresistible Force meets the Immovable Object.

The antagonist need not be a person, but there is usually a character who fulfils a major role of opposition for the protagonist; Michael Hauge refers to this as the *nemesis*. In *Body Heat*, Racine's nemesis is Matty's husband, but unknown to him, his real antagonist is Matty. Inspector Clouseau's nemesis is not Charles Lytton, the Pink Panther, but his own superior, Dreyfus. Clarice Starling's nemesis is not Buffalo Bill, but Hannibal Lecter. McCauley's nemesis is not Hanna, but Waingro.

Forces Of Antagonism

The antagonistic force may be killer shark (*Jaws*), epidemic (*Outbreak*), disease (*My Life*), accident (*Regarding Henry*), disaster (*The Towering Inferno*), act of God (*Earthquake*), alien organism (*Invasion Of The Body Snatchers*), corrupt corporation (*The Insider*), corrupt political body (*All The President's Men*); anything that provides the protagonist with a set of obstacles to surmount. In *The Full Monty* it is the hopeless system the characters are trapped in, and the social and economic hardships they are struggling to overcome. The narrative provides no long-term solution to their problems but they do transcend them for a few precious minutes of elation and achievement. In *The Straight Story* it is the sheer scale and absurdity of Alvin's self-appointed task. In *American Beauty* it is society; the reaction of the other characters to Lester's all too successful attempts to break free from the constraints of marriage, the rat race and stifling middle-class inertia. In *The Terminator* it is a virtually indestructible cybernetic killing machine. In *The Long Good Friday*, Harold spends most of the narrative trying to discover who is at war with him, and why.

Only Connect

You will of course have other major characters who play key roles in your story. They often follow certain types but take care to avoid clumsy stereotypes. Do not treat them as if they were straight out of central casting - give them the same vitality and depth as your hero and villain. Characters exist in their own right and in relation to others. The protagonist often has a good friend, or helper; also possibly the aforementioned nemesis, and a romantic interest - sometimes shared by the antagonist. In a good script, these relationships form a complex web rather than a bunch of loose ends. Characters connect through their (inner) needs, (outer) desires, problems, ghosts and fears. The more levels on which your characters connect, the tighter and more satisfying your script will be, and the greater its connection with readers.

Example: *American Beauty*

American Beauty is a must-see movie for any aspiring screenwriter, brilliantly connecting characters on many levels. The motivations, desires, problems and ghosts of each character are echoed in the other characters. Also the narrative subverts expectations - we expect Carolyn to be Lester's nemesis, we expect Lester to have sex with Angela, we expect Colonel Fitts to confront Lester, but certainly not in the way he does. The fears of each character have connections: Lester fears crushing social and personal torpor; Carolyn fears failure, loss of status and the crumbling family façade; Jane fears being ordinary, not belonging and family breakdown; Ricky fears his father discovering his drug dealing; Angela fears being ordinary, her lies being discovered and her own sexuality; Frank fears that the world is not ordinary and that his son is homosexual, echoing his shame over his own military experiences.

The film connects with a large audience because the characters are 'real' and they want what we all want; *life on our own terms*. The delicious irony is that in the course of the narrative only Lester accomplishes this, and he pays the ultimate price for doing so.

Exercise: Study the connections and interrelationships between characters in three films of your choice. Construct a table with columns for Motivations/ Needs, Desires, Problems, Fears and Ghost for each character in each film, leaving no blanks. Then do one for your own script when it's ready.

Whose Story?

Whose story are you telling? You may think you know who your protagonist is, but take a pause for reflection. Perhaps the story is more interesting from the perspective of another character. Is the point of view of the victim more dramatic than that of the cop? Rather than showing the family saga via the tyrannical father, might it be better to view him through the frightened eyes of his daughter or son, or the wife and mother caught in the middle? Think it through and centralise the character who facilitates the best structure, the most tension, the highest drama and who elicits the greatest emotional response from the reader. A tip: sketch every scene from the perspective of each character in it - what are their objectives in the scene, and how will the outcome affect their motivations and problems? The character you are most interested in should be your Protagonist.

Character Intros

Some screenwriters include short character introductions. Paul Schrader's sketch of Travis Bickle in *Taxi Driver* is one of the best:

```
Age 26, lean, hard, the consummate loner. On the surface he
appears good-looking, even handsome; he has a quiet, steady
look and a disarming smile which flashes from nowhere, light-
ing up his whole face. But behind that smile, around his dark
eyes, in his gaunt cheeks, one can see the ominous stains
caused by a life of private fear, emptiness and loneliness. He
seems to have wandered in from a land where it is always cold,
a country where the inhabitants seldom speak. The head moves,
the expression changes, but the eyes remain ever-fixed,
unblinking, piercing empty space. (...) He has the smell of
sex about him: Sick sex, repressed sex, lonely sex, but sex
nonetheless. He is a raw male force driving forward; toward
what, one cannot tell. Then one looks closer and sees the
inevitable. The clock spring cannot be wound continually
tighter. As the earth moves toward the sun, Travis Bickle
moves toward violence.
```

Brilliant, immediate and disturbing. If you know your Protagonist as well as Schrader, and can profile him with as much impact, then you'll have few problems.

In *Heat*, Michael Mann profiles all his major characters. Here's one:

INT. "TOYS 'R' US" STORE - ON CERRITO - DAY

```
MICHAEL CERRITO - at 40 - is looking at a doll house. He's a
wide, thick, coarse-featured big man. Sicilian from Sunnyside,
he's spent 15 years in Attica, Joliet and Marion penitentia-
ries. He's strictly a "cowboy": his natural inclination
towards a score is "...get the guns and let's go." He's been
off smack and everything else for five years. He's clean and
sober. He's the nicest guy on the block and a loving father.
If you get in his way, he'll kill you as soon as look at you.
If you asked him about the contradictions, he wouldn't know
what you were talking about.
```

Only do this if you're confident that it (and the rest of your script) is good enough.

Character Arc

An overarching arc represents your protagonist's journey through the narrative, from and to equilibrium (back in the normal world or a new one in the special world), with the turning point coming at the mid-point. It is a device to keep your focus on the essential elements of character - needs, wants, motivations, fears, problems. Writers constantly digress, so if you've written a scene which does not connect with the essential elements of the character, or does not move him forward, then cut it. No matter how much you may like the scene, the farther it moves away from the character arc, the more important it is that you lose it.

True Character

We know characters by actions rather than words; most notably how they react under pressure. Anyone can be a saint when things are going well. True character is only revealed in adversity, so put your characters in danger, often. Different types of danger bring different kinds of response - how do they react to physical danger, or loss of status and career, or psychological pressure? As you've seen, credibility and consistency are also important factors here. When Harold Shand discovers the IRA are behind the campaign against him, his fighting character determines his actions - he refuses to accept the odds and takes the fight to them, with disastrous consequences.

Character Traits & Accessories

Consistent and memorable traits are the hallmark of three-dimensional characters; from little quirks to deep-rooted and revealing aspects of their personality. Even short catchphrases work as character signatures: The Emperor's "There it is!" in *Amadeus*, Derek Vinyard's "What were you thinking?" in *American History X* and Annie's "La-di-dah" in *Annie Hall*.

In *Heat*, McCauley's primary trait is his zen-like emotional detachment; the discipline to drop everything and leave in 30 seconds flat if he feels the heat around the corner. Yet when he is finally in a position to get clean away, his discipline fails and his true desire for revenge on Waingro takes him back into the situation from which he had escaped. Charles Morse's encyclopedic knowledge of trivia is pitted against his nemesis' he-man persona to see whose trait will be more useful in their fight for survival against the elements. Dave Wilson's key trait is his astonishing compulsion to act on irrational impulse against the odds. Bridget Gregory's is her sharp, calculating, manipulative manner, not her minor mirror-writing ability.

Accessories also help flesh out a character, and can be memorable in their own right. Charles Bronson's character in *Once Upon A Time In The West* always announces his presence by playing a plaintive harmonica riff. Look at the numerous uses for Indiana Jones' whip. In 1955 Film Noir *The Big Combo*, a hearing aid worn by Richard Conte's henchman is removed when he is about to be shot. Seen from his POV, the guns' muzzle flares erupt in total silence.

Five Great Character Movies:

All About My Mother; *Raiders Of The Lost Ark*; *American Beauty*; *Sexy Beast*; *Diva*.

Dialogue

"When the screenplay has been written and the dialogue has been added, we're ready to shoot."

Alfred Hitchcock (Screenwriter/Director)

First Things Last

Dialogue is one of the major blind alleys that fledgling screenwriters love to run headlong into. When asked how their script is going, they'll say "Great." When asked what they've got so far, they'll say "A couple of good characters and lots of nice dialogue." Translation: almost nothing. No beginning/middle/end story, no clearly defined needs/wants/problems for their Protagonist, no synopsis, just dialogue. Never begin by writing dialogue. How can you know what your characters will say to each other until you place them within a plot structure and know what they will be reacting to or setting up? Until you know their goals, their problems and their objectives in each scene?

Film is about action and visuals, theatre is about dialogue. Screenwriting is about showing, not telling. Students often find it hard to adjust to the fact that dialogue is edited to the bone, and the more action-based the premise, the more the dialogue is dictated by the demands of the plot. Even character-based scripts require no more dialogue than it takes to accomplish characters' immediate objectives. Know your story events and build your plot outline first, think about dialogue last.

Less Is More

Dialogue is minimalist in nature. A question is often followed by a question, and tension is conveyed through the thrust and parry of pared-down, to-the-point argument and disagreement. Read a few scripts. You'll notice that there are very few large blocks of dialogue. Mostly it is a line or two followed by a line or two, all the way down a page.

The first thing to ask yourself about each piece of dialogue is "Can I cut a word without losing anything?" Next question: "Can I cut a line?" Next: "Can I cut the whole piece and give the same information visually?" If yes, then do so. Visual before aural, every time.

Directness is often best. If your character Lisa's new boyfriend Matt hasn't called her for a while, and she sees him in the street, here's what she *shouldn't* say:

```
                LISA
      Er, hi Matt. Ah, look, I was
      just wondering why, you know,
      you haven't contacted me and,
      well, I really miss you and--
```

To a reader her character appears weak and uninteresting, and your dialogue appalling. Think about her motivation in the scene.

```
                LISA
      So. Matthew. Where do I stand?
```

This is better. Simple and direct, in control, fulfilling her objective, putting the onus on Matt to find a good answer. Maybe better still would be:

```
Matt advances towards her, a big grin on his lips. As he
reaches her, arms open wide, she...

neatly sidesteps him and strides past, without a backward
glance.
```

There are many variations. She could slap him, grab and kiss an unsuspecting passer-by - anything is better than that first piece of dialogue. Positive action and decision-making endear characters to audiences.

No Conversation

Film writing excludes meandering, conversational dialogue. What may sound like conversation isn't, unless you're Quentin Tarantino and can get away with it because your ear for the rhythms of dialogue is so good. I'm assuming you're not, so each line should add weight to your character and reflect their scene objectives. Make it intriguing, memorable and delicious.

Example: *Things To Do In Denver When You're Dead*

In the following extract from Scott Rosenberg's script *Things To Do In Denver When You're Dead*, Jimmy The Saint is in a bar for happy hour. It's been a bad day. His business partner gives him financial news that makes it worse still. But Jimmy's attention is distracted. Across the room he spies an incredibly beautiful woman sitting at a table with her friends, and everything else leaves his mind. He moves in a straight line, eyes fixed on her face, zeroing in on her table. She looks up, makes eye contact and looks away, blushing at his intensity. CUT TO: The woman leans against a pillar, faux-nonchalantly, as Jimmy gazes into her eyes:

47

<pre>
              JIMMY
   Dagny? That's your name?
   Tremendous name. My name's
   Jimmy. And I just have one
   simple, impulsive question. Are
   you in love?

              DAGNY
   What?

              JIMMY
   At the present time, are you in
   love?

              DAGNY
   Why?

              JIMMY
   Because if you are then I won't
   waste your time. I'm really not
   the type of man to impede
   another man's happiness. However,
   if you're not presently in love
   then I will continue my rhapsody
   because if I may say so Dagny,
   you are most definitely the
   bee's knees.
</pre>

How much better is this than simply asking her to dinner? She is flattered
despite her reservations, and intrigued, as are we. She admits that there is someone in her life:

<pre>
              DAGNY
   We date; I have memorised his
   phone number but I won't use his
   toothbrush. We're somewhere in
   between-- and he's crazy about me.

              JIMMY
   As he should be. You glide.

              DAGNY
   I glide?

              JIMMY
   You glide. It's a very attractive
   quality. Most girls, they merely
   plod along-- you, on the other
   hand, you glide.
</pre>

She has memorised his phone number but won't use his toothbrush. Rather
than talking around the subject, her dialogue goes straight to the heart of it with

this beautiful, razor-sharp line. Jimmy keeps up his impetus, matter-of-factly asking if her boyfriend makes her "thump."

                    DAGNY
          Define "thump".

                    JIMMY
          Thump. When you think about him
          you can't sleep, when he smiles
          you forget about man's
          inhumanity to man, does he do
          that for you--

                    DAGNY
          That's a ridiculous concept. No
          one can do that for--

                    JIMMY
          Girls who glide need guys who
          make them thump.

The charm of this scene is unbelievable. The characters' objectives are basic - Jimmy wants Dagny to agree to have dinner with him; Dagny wants to assess whether Jimmy has a personality behind the rap before giving an answer. On the surface it seems nothing out of the ordinary, but the scintillating dialogue is there to be savoured and to hook the reader.

Again, like all good scenes, this one is multifunctional. When Jimmy achieves his objective and leaves the bar on a high, he is immediately accosted by The Man With The Plan's goons who want him to go with them. This is consistent with the rhythm of screenplays - highs followed by lows, interiors followed by exteriors, noise followed by quiet; in short, different types of contrasts between scenes. It also serves to give Jimmy something to make him vulnerable, something to lose. His business is failing, so that won't do. But Dagny really is the bee's knees, and his feelings for her drive his later actions when his mistakes place her in danger.

Dos & Don'ts

Do:
- Make it memorable - obvious, banal or lumpen dialogue litters most scripts I read.
- Ensure each character's dialogue connects with their scene objectives.
- Ask yourself whether every line could be better.
- Ask yourself whether every line could be shorter. Can you can lose words, or whole sentences? A tip: if you want to lose a piece of dialogue, try cutting the beginning and the end. You may find the middle contains the essence of your objective.

- Ask yourself whether you could achieve your objectives visually. In *Citizen Kane*, Welles conveyed Kane and Emily's marriage breakdown by cutting most of the dialogue and simply showing their breakfast becoming more estranged each time - sitting further away from each other, body language, reading different newspapers etc.

- Make each character stand out. Reinforce their personality (actions) by what they say and give them individual voices rather than your own.

- Remember that dialogue is mainly shaped in the redrafting stage, and will be extensively reworked after you've sold the script, either by yourself or someone else.

Don't:

- Direct actors. Avoid parenthetical instructions on how to say the words and let actors do their job.

- Include dialect or stammers or accents. Indicate them in the blackstuff (scene description).

- Include page-long monologues or huge chunks of back-and-forth philosophising. Any longer pieces can be broken up by interjecting scene description details - movements, comings and goings etc. If you do have monologues or longer passages, make sure every word is worth its place. Billy Bob Thornton's *Sling Blade* script is a good example.

- Forget the subtext. Allow dialogue to be read against its real meaning to give depth to characters, and allow small things to symbolise larger things.

- Deviate from the essence of the character, in mode or content of speech.

Five Great Dialogue Movies:

Things To Do In Denver When You're Dead; *Apocalypse Now*; *House Of Games*; *Heat*; *Naked*.

7. Structure & Format

"Screenplays are structure"

William Goldman (Screenwriter)

Structure

Classic Hollywood Narrative System (CHNS)

The foundations of screenplay construction were laid in the early days of Hollywood (albeit appropriated from well-established principles of mythology and narrative) and have since remained largely intact. A screenplay tells a visual story in which plot events follow a rigid internal logic of cause and effect so that the audience knows what is happening to whom and why. As discussed in chapter 6, the plot normally pivots around the protagonist, a dynamic central character with clear needs, desires and problems who encounters an antagonistic force while in pursuit of his goals. His attempts to overcome this opposition as he undergoes a life-changing series of events drive the narrative, building to a climax where he emerges victorious but also mindful of how close he came to defeat and of what he learned along the way. Modern variations are surprise, downbeat and/or ambiguous endings, where the protagonist either snatches defeat from the jaws of success, fails miserably or loses so much in reaching his goal that it brings the wisdom of the whole enterprise into question. Syd Field has advised against such endings but when done well they are among the most memorable examples of cinema: *Chinatown, Apocalypse Now, Seven, Get Carter, The Long Good Friday, The Vanishing* (original) and *The Wages Of Fear.*

Art-Film Narrative

Art-film narrative was mainly developed in European cinema as a form of cultural opposition to the dominant Hollywood model; more open to experiment and idiosyncrasy, its appeal is limited to a narrower audience. Examples include *A bout de souffle, L'Avventura, A Zed And Two Noughts, Last Year At Marienbad* and *The Idiots.* Art-film conventions allow character motivations to be opaque and confusing, events to abandon a cause and effect relationship, narrative strands to be oblique or remain deliberately unresolved, visual artifice and style to take precedence over plot coherence and viewers to arrive at their own understanding of meaning among multiple possibilities. Some of my favourite films ingeniously combine elements of Art-film narrative with CHNS: *Blue Velvet, Diva, Subway, Run Lola Run, Barton Fink, The Reflecting Skin, Trust, Toto The Hero, The Fourth Man, Exotica, The Limey, Requiem For A Dream.*

Three-Act Structure

If, as I said in chapter 6, the Protagonist is the vehicle that carries the reader through the narrative, then structure is your road map for him. The framework supporting CHNS is a three-act beginning/middle/end screenplay (although acts are not formally separated) in which the middle act is roughly twice the length of the first and last acts. Using the principle that one page of properly formatted script equals one minute of screen time, this equates to 30 minutes/60 minutes/30 minutes for a two-hour screenplay.

An old Hollywood maxim goes: Get your hero up a tree, throw rocks at him, and then get him down again. In his book *A Pound Of Flesh*, producer Art Linson relates how 'David Mamet, in attempting to explain the three-act theory, said that he read a news headline in the *New York Post* which declared, 'Boy Cuts Off Father's Head, Cuts Off Parakeet's Head, Then Cuts Off Lizard's Head.' He said the secret is to tell the screenwriter to cut the father's head off last.'

Films within genres that usually run over two hours, like sprawling epics, biopics or adaptations of classic novels, require more acts to underpin the length; *Lawrence Of Arabia* has seven. Films incorporating art narrative may play around with structure; *Full Metal Jacket* and *She's Gotta Have It* have two acts. Ken Dancyger & Jeff Rush contend that *Mean Streets* has only one. David Siegel breaks 90% of films that have broken the $100 million mark at the US box office into his own nine-act structure. John Truby runs courses based on his 22-step structure. Beware of treating act structure as a formula; it's not. There is no such thing as a formula for writing a screenplay, merely a suggested form.

The three-act model has never met a sustained commercial or theoretical challenge and continues to hold sway, but that doesn't mean you *have* to use it. However, as a first-timer, if your screenplay is constructed within an accepted architecture it shows that you have researched the craft in a professional manner. And in the megadollar-driven world of film production, this model has been proven to reach the widest audience and therefore return the largest profit.

The timeline for three-act structure looks like this:

Opening Sequence

Or, the First Ten Pages. Script readers have developed a professional short-hand based around the opening and closing ten pages and dialogue samples, to enable them to cope with the sheer volume of scripts they have to wade through. If your opening is weak, your climax will probably also fail to deliver. If so, your script is dead in the water. I read far too many scripts which open with some character interaction and dialogue, but without any real incident to generate and sustain interest. You must pique the reader's interest from the beginning. The primary requirement for your script's opening sequence is to hit the ground running, either literally or metaphorically - Something Must Happen. The Inciting

52

Incident inserts the Hook under readers' skins, stimulates their excitement and gets them emotionally involved with the Protagonist and his problem.

The essential elements of a strong opening are: introduce at least one major character (usually the Protagonist and/or Antagonist); set the tone (mood/atmosphere); set the pace; and introduce the world of the story via a powerful incident or situation which sets in motion the events of the plot.

Example: *The Last Seduction*

The opening of Steve Barancik's script (originally titled *Buffalo Girls*):

```
INT. BOILER ROOM - DAY

Light glints off a vintage U.S. silver dollar. THE CAMERA
PULLS BACK TO REVEAL: a high-pressure phone sales operation.
Many small desks crammed into a space. Mostly men at various
stages of their "pitch". You RING a BELL when you make a sale
-- someone does every ten seconds or so. The product: a "rare,
commemorative coin set." The room hums. Everyone smokes.

The owner, in a tiny office, oversees the action. Small and
pinched-looking, he watches closely.

Bitch-goddess-ringmaster BRIDGET GREGORY, late twenties,
strolls among the reps with a stack of ten-dollar bills. When
a BELL RINGS, the rep hands her a sales slip and she hands him
a bill. She's well dressed but no one dares look. She wears a
wireless mike.
```

And later on the same page:

```
A tightly clenched fist grips the handle of a cheap briefcase.
THE CAMERA PULLS BACK TO REVEAL: CLAY GREGORY, a good-looking
man about thirty walking quickly through an unfamiliar neigh-
borhood in New York City. He's obviously on edge. He crosses
without pause at an intersection, making a car come to a skid-
ding halt. The IRRITATED DRIVER lays on the horn and Clay
flips him off and continues on his way.
```

The story world is introduced visually, using brief sentences and simple language. The tone is tense and vaguely unpleasant, reflecting the nature of events in the plot. The pace is clipped and brisk, echoing the tempo of the plot and suggesting an editing rhythm. The characters take the stage: Bridget Gregory ('Bitch-goddess-ringmaster,' 'She's well dressed but no one dares look') and her husband Clay ('...a good-looking man about thirty...') These economical sketches establish right away who is the most important, and intriguing, character. The inciting incident comes on page five: Clay risks his life for a drug deal worth hundreds of thousands of dollars, but we soon learn that Bridget is the brains behind it:

```
                    CLAY (CONT'D)
          You're a criminal mastermind.

                    BRIDGET
          It's only a hobby.
```

Page nine: while Clay showers, Bridget writes him a note which he can only read in front of a mirror, puts condoms in her purse and flees with the money. Remember that character is revealed more by actions than words. Bridget is scheming and manipulative, uses her sexuality to get what she wants and is more than a match for guys like Clay. A simple set-up keeps us asking questions: What is her plan? Will she stay ahead of him? Will he get his revenge and the money? Which gullible guy will she find next? What is the significance of her mirror-writing trait? Questions engage readers and keep them turning pages to find out what happens next.

Exercise: Watch three of your favourite films and analyse how their openings follow, or deviate from, conventions of structure and character. Read a few scripts for films you haven't seen and do the same. Watch the opening ten minutes of *Quiz Show*, *The Insider*, *Three Colours Blue*, *Body Heat* and *Heavy*. Analyse similarities and differences in the way each narrative tells the story. What is the inciting incident in each case? How do you think the story will develop? Were you right?

Act I: Set-Up/Situation/Establishment

The first quarter of the script sets up the plot world via the main characters' relationships and situations, supplies most of the relevant backstory and delivers the crucial Inciting Incident. This usually occurs at or near the start. It provides the impetus and/or context for the plot and, directly or indirectly, provides the hero with his Problem or Task:

- In *Body Heat*, Racine meets Matty and is immediately hooked.
- In *Jaws*, the shark makes its first kill and Brody begins his investigation.
- In *Alien*, Mother revives the Nostromo's crew to investigate the distress signal from the alien ship.
- In *Seven*, Mills and Somerset's partnership gets off to a bad start (almost a rule - partners hate each other at the outset) and John Doe's first murder lets them know this is going to be unlike anything they've known before.
- In *American Beauty*, Lester decides it's not too late to get back what he's lost, just as the Fitts are moving in next door.
- In *Heat*, Waingro compromises the security van heist and attracts major police heat for the guards' murders.
- In *The Player*, Griffin receives his first threatening postcard.

- In *Citizen Kane*, Kane dies, setting in motion Thompson's quest to find the meaning of his final word, "Rosebud."

1st Act Watershed

Or Plot Point 1, or Turning Point 1 (or, confusingly, Inciting Incident, because of its direct impact on the protagonist's life). This is a major climactic event which spins both protagonist and plot into the unknown quantity of Act II. In a 120-page script, this normally occurs around page 25-29, allowing the second act to begin on or near page 30.

- In *Body Heat*, Racine hurls the chair through Matty's window because he has to have her.
- In *The Edge*, Morse's seaplane goes down in the river.
- In *Silence Of The Lambs*, Buffalo Bill kidnaps the senator's daughter and Clarice is summoned to join the investigation.
- In *Alien*, Kane is attacked by the facehugger and, despite Ripley's quarantine order, is brought back on board the Nostromo.
- In *Seven*, Mills investigates John Doe's third murder on his own after Somerset withdraws from the case.

Contrary to some opinions, act structure is not a recent innovation, nor is it confined to 'lowbrow' movies. Most films that aim to attract a large audience adopt it. Alfred Hitchcock's playfully exaggerated normal/special world watershed in *North By Northwest* is one of my favourites: Roger Thornhill goes to the United Nations building to confront Lester Townsend. First, he discovers that Townsend is not the man who had him abducted, then when Vandamm's henchman kills Townsend from off-screen, a large crowd witnesses Roger standing over the body holding the knife. The final flourish arrives with a press photographer's flash, capturing the moment for tomorrow's front pages as Roger flees into Act II, now wanted for murder.

Act II: Complication/Development/Plot

Most of the actual plot occurs during this hour or so, developing the events set in motion in Act I and building to the resolution. In pursuing his goal, the protagonist has to surmount progressively more difficult obstacles and complications, which arrive thicker and faster. It is crucial that you accelerate the pace, raise the stakes and build intensity and action. Many spec scripts run out of steam and become boring at this point. Again the act closes with a major setback, requiring the protagonist to muster all his resources for Act III.

1st Focus Point

Every successful script has a rhythm, and the peaks and troughs of rhythm are linked to the structural 'shape.' Breaking an act of sixty minutes down into four roughly equal parts is an exercise in rhythm and structure. About 15 minutes into act II, on or around page 45, a Focus Point (or to use Syd Field's term, *pinch*) loops around the protagonist's problem and the plot, and draws both lines taut. This key scene focuses readers' attention back on the protagonist's problem and shows him coming to terms with the nature/magnitude of his task in the special world, *or* shows another character's action that will, either deliberately or by accident, do him a favour (ladder) or cause him further complications (snake).

- In *Body Heat*, Matty says aloud what she knows Racine is thinking: life would be fine if her husband were dead. Racine vows to kill him.

- In *Alien*, the facehugger's blood corrodes the deck when Ash tries to remove it from Kane, prompting Parker's great line: "Wonderful defence mechanism - you don't dare kill it."

- In *Silence Of The Lambs*, Clarice's find from Bill's victim's throat is identified as a Death's Head moth, providing her first significant lead.

- In *Seven*, Somerset discovers 'Help Me' written in fingerprints on the wall; the police think the prints reveal John Doe's identity, but Somerset remains skeptical.

Mid-Point/Point Of No Return

Effectively, the mid-point provides another Plot Point around the halfway mark which breaks the 60-page act into two main units and introduces another kind of watershed for the protagonist, often changing his direction and massively raising the stakes. It is also known as The Point Of No Return because after this incident, there is no going back.

- In *Body Heat*, Racine murders Matty's husband.

- In *Seven*, Mills and Somerset discover, chase and then lose John Doe.

- In *Alien*, the creature bursts from Kane's chest and escapes into the bowels of the ship.

- In *Silence Of The Lambs*, Lecter is taken from jail to meet the senator, furthering his master plan and threatening Clarice's career.

- In *The Crying Game*, Fergus discovers Dil's 'secret.'

2nd Focus Point

The second Focus Point performs a similar function for the second half of Act II as the first focus point does for the first half. On or around page 75, another key scene tightens (pinches) the focus on the protagonist's complications, often echoing or paying off the first focus point.

- In *Body Heat*, Matty's husband's glasses are missed and the heat is turned up on Racine as rumours spread.

- In *Silence Of The Lambs*, Clarice finally bares her soul to Lecter, and when she leaves the jail he immediately stages his breakout.

- In *Alien*, the creature's new seven-feet-tall form is revealed as it picks off engineer Brett.

- In *Seven*, John Doe telephones his apartment and tells Mills that his biggest surprise is still to come.

2nd Act Watershed

Bad things happen. The Protagonist often ends act II on a real low, seemingly very far from achieving his goal or completing his task.

- In *Body Heat*, Racine realises that he's being set up by someone and he doesn't have any answers.

- In *Silence Of The Lambs*, Clarice realises that Lecter's cryptic message means Buffalo Bill knew his first victim, but she is removed from the investigation and suspended from the Academy.

- In *Alien*, the creature kills Dallas, the ship's captain. What can the remaining crew do against this indestructible killing machine?

- In *Seven*, John Doe calmly walks in to the police station and gives himself up, but only to put the last part of his plan into action.

Act III: Climax & Resolution/Conclusion

After mentally and/or physically pulling himself together, the protagonist shakes off the low at the end of Act II and gains a new impetus towards a grand finale, where usually he finally achieves his goal, the force of opposition is vanquished and the loose ends (sub-plots) are tied.

- In *Silence Of The Lambs*, the FBI are on a wild goose chase while Clarice finds herself triumphant after her nightmare battle in Buffalo Bill's house.

- In *Alien*, Ripley, last survivor of the Nostromo, lies in hypersleep after ejecting the creature into space and blasting it with the drive jets.

- In *The Player*, Griffin purchases his anonymous nemesis' pitch of his own scenario, thereby securing the writer's movie deal and his own future.

The protagonist doesn't always have a happy end.

- In *Body Heat*, Racine is behind bars and Matty is living it up on a beach with hunk in tow.

- In *Seven*, John Doe's 'present' sends Mills over the edge. By executing Doe, he also performs the final deadly sin: murder.

- In *The Long Good Friday*, the amazing final held close-up of Harold's face as he's driven away at gunpoint speaks volumes about his emotions, knowing he's about to die because he refused to accept that he couldn't win.

Now let's examine a movie in detail to see how this all fits together.

Case Study In Structure: *Crimson Tide*

Synopsis: When rebels commandeer a Russian naval base and threaten to launch ICBMs against America, nuclear sub USS Alabama is deployed as first line of defence. On board, the relationship between young, thoughtful Executive Officer Ron Hunter and hardass veteran Captain Frank Ramsey gets off to a shaky start. When the Alabama's radio antenna is cut during an attack by a Russian sub, an Emergency Action Message is interrupted. Did the message confirm or countermand an earlier order to launch a nuclear strike? Ramsey proceeds with the launch, but Hunter refuses to give his assent until the message can be verified. When Ramsey threatens to launch anyway, Hunter relieves him of command. Crew members loyal to Ramsey take steps to counter this move. With the clock counting down to a possible global holocaust, each man must choose his side...

Opening Sequence: Inciting Incident: The Russian rebels' takeover of the base. Live from a US aircraft carrier, a CNN news anchor reports the worsening situation and the nuclear threat posed to America.

Backstory/character development: While Hunter's daughter's birthday party is in full swing, he and colleague 'Weps' watch events unfold on TV. The phone rings - their call-up. Hunter is interviewed by Ramsey, whose usual XO (Executive Officer) has appendicitis. The contrast is immediate: Hunter is philosophical; Ramsey is Navy to the bone. Hunter is a family man; Ramsey is a loner with a Jack Russell terrier for a constant companion. Hunter is a man of few words; Ramsey is opinionated and judgmental. After Ramsey's dog takes a liking to him, Hunter gets the assignment.

(10 minutes) Hunter says goodbye to his family and joins the Alabama.

Watershed 1 (29 minutes): First major conflict: Hunter is fighting a fire in the galley when Ramsey calls a weapons drill. Hunter questions his timing. Ramsey aborts the drill when a crewman dies from injuries sustained in the fire. Summoned to Ramsey's quarters, Hunter restates his disagreement with the decision. Ramsey tells him to wait for a private moment if he has anything to say and in the meantime to keep his fucking mouth shut: "We're here to preserve democracy, not practise it."

1st Focus Point (47 minutes): Conflicting ideologies: Hunter wants the full text of the Emergency Action Message (EAM) but the sub is too deep for radio contact and can't surface because a potentially hostile Russian sub is in the vicinity. Annoyed, Ramsey accedes to Hunter's request to float the radio buoy, but the winch sounds on sonar and gives away the Alabama's position. The Russian sub attacks. Ramsey blames Hunter.

Mid-Point (58 minutes): Chewable tension: Hunter refuses to confirm Ramsey's order to launch weapons until the attack damage can be repaired and the EAM confirmed. Ramsey threatens to get someone else to do it. Citing Navy regulations, Hunter relieves him of his command and has him confined to quarters.

2ⁿᵈ Focus Point (75 minutes): Echoes the first FP conflict: Weps, the only man who can access the second set of launch keys, is recruited to Ramsey's mutiny against Hunter, after being convinced that the Russians are about to launch and that the real mutiny was Hunter's.

2ⁿᵈ Watershed (90 minutes): Told by Hunter that the decision to fire is his alone, Weps can't carry out Ramsey's order to remove the tactical firing trigger. Ramsey pulls a gun, but shooting Weps would render launch impossible, so points it at his colleague instead...

Climax (95-100 minutes): Knife-edge: Stand-off between the two factions as Ramsey gives the engineer three minutes to repair the radio until the Russian missiles are fuelled and the Alabama launches hers. In the nick of time the repair is completed. The EAM comes through with orders to abandon launch because the rebels have surrendered. The crew cheers. Ramsey hands command to Hunter and goes to his quarters.

Resolution (105 minutes): Ambiguous. A high-level naval disciplinary panel delivers its verdict on the events on board the Alabama. It finds that under strict Navy protocol, they were both right - and both wrong. The fact that this situation could arise has given Navy command a huge headache. Ramsey retires from service and Hunter is given his own command.

Utilizing Structure

The ongoing debate among writers over the merits or drawbacks of three-act structure rages on, so let me be clear: I'm not saying you must use it, and certainly never at the expense of creativity and originality. My advice to novice screenwriters is: utilise it, at least for your first script, or learn it inside-out before you attempt to depart from it. Let me give you a final example.

Example: *Being John Malkovich*

Recently a student copied me an interview with Charlie Kaufman, writer of *Being John Malkovich*, in which he said "I think one of the reasons I talked about my [writing] process at all is because I've been so angered by these courses in screenwriting and Hollywood's endorsement of them, treating a piece of writing as a product as opposed to an exploration." My student's point was that something as one-off as *Malkovich* can't be confined within structural norms, and finds its own form outside of them. So I reread the script, and here's what I found:

Opening Sequence (pages 1-10): Protagonist Craig Schwartz, after a series of setbacks, is forced to take a job he doesn't want because there's no demand for his skills as a puppeteer. This is a classic square peg in round hole situation.

1st Watershed (page 30): Looking for cards he dropped behind a filing cabinet, Craig discovers a portal directly into the mind of John Malkovich. He tells his colleague Maxine, "I don't think I can go on living my life as I have lived it." This is a classic normal world/special world scenario.

1st Focus Point (page 45): Looking through Malkovich's eyes, Craig's wife Lotte lusts after Maxine and plans to vicariously make love to her through him.

Mid-Point (page 56): Craig ambushes Lotte and goes into Malkovich in her place, to make love to Maxine.

2nd Focus Point (page 75): Maxine makes love to Malkovich despite knowing it's Craig inside, not Lotte.

2nd Watershed (page 86): Craig, now in total control of Malkovich, fills in the portal and announces he is quitting acting for a new career as a puppeteer.

Climax (page 101): Lester kidnaps and threatens to kill Maxine, forcing Craig to surrender control of Malkovich to his group.

Resolution (page 109): Ambiguous. POV of Maxine's seven-year-old daughter Emily (or is it Craig?) as, inside Malkovich, Lester's group plans their transfer to the new vessel...

Charlie Kaufman is a fine writer but, brilliant and original as *Being John Malkovich* is, I found the script as recognisably and logically structured as *Crimson Tide* - not as a "product," but because an effective framework can support even "exploratory" stories. Think of act structure as a scaffold for your script, not as a straitjacket, and use it accordingly.

Scenes & Sequences

The smallest unit of dramatic action is a Scene. A scene transition occurs whenever there is a change of location and/or time. Your individual scenes should come alive on the page, and function individually in addition to connecting with others. Scenes are driven by character motivations and plot advancement. Try to give each scene a beginning, middle and end, and leave readers asking questions about what will happen next. Establish your characters' objectives for each scene and cut anything that does not contribute to them.

A collection of thematically linked scenes forms a Sequence. You can title such sequences: the Odessa Steps sequence (*Battleship Potemkin*), the chariot race sequence (*Ben-Hur*) etc.

One of my favourites is the audacious 20-minute 'Poker Game' sequence (which also builds to a first act climax and provides a glorious reversal) in *House Of Games*: At the House of Games, Dr Margaret Ford agrees to Mike's proposal that if she sits in the poker game, he'll tear up her suicidal client's $800 marker. Mike is losing heavily to a Vegas hustler and Margaret is to look for the guy's "tell" - when he's bluffing, he plays with his gold ring but he knows Mike has caught him and he's stopped.

Finally, in a hand worth $6000, Mike has three aces. He leaves to go to the toilet. Margaret watches as the hustler fiddles with his ring, just as predicted. When Mike returns, she whispers that the guy's bluffing and he must call the bet. Mike has a problem - he doesn't have the cash and needs a marker. The guy gets mad and insists that if Mike can't call the bet he'll have to fold the hand. Margaret calls the bet and says she'll write a cheque if Mike loses, knowing of course that he won't. The guy doesn't like it but the other players agree. Mike triumphantly flips his three aces... and then... the hustler fans out a club flush! Stunned faces around the table, not least Margaret's. Mike is furious, and demands to know how the fuck the guy got a flush after he did the tell. The hustler goes apeshit and places a gun on the table, demanding his $6000. The tension is electric.

Margaret takes out her cheque book and begins to write, focusing on the gun... as a bead of water drips from the barrel. She tears up the cheque. The players back off; the hustler is apoplectic. She tells him he can't threaten her with a squirt gun. He protests but Mike tells him "George, you've blown the gaff." Tension is released ingeniously with humour as George says "I told you a goddamn squirt gun wouldn't work." Mike tells him it would have worked fine; he didn't have to *fill* it. The audience's laughter usually drowns George's reply: "What, I'm going to threaten someone with an empty gun?" Margaret is incredulous. They insist "It's nothing personal," "It's only business." One born every minute, and two to take 'em. Mike gives her a chip as a souvenir of her visit and she can't help laughing. Her normal world has somersaulted into the special world.

Format

"Screenplay form is simple; so simple, in fact, that most people try to make it more complex"

Syd Field

"You should write a movie as if you were describing a finished film to a blind person."

Gill Dennis (Screenwriting Lecturer)

Screenplay Format

Screenwriters love to debate the pros and cons of screenplay format. Some think that having a prescribed layout for a script is a good thing; others find it restrictive and insist on going their own way. Some centre character cues, others place them at the left indent. Some use professional software packages, some use tabs on their word processor, some make it up as they go along.

My advice is: stop the debate - *it ain't optional*. The industry has clear expectations - rules by any other name - about the format for submitted screenplays. If you write a script with intent to impress, progress and sell, then you'd better abide by them. Submitting a screenplay in a non-standard format marks your card as unprofessional in an industry that has the luxury of demanding professionalism from writers because it's a buyer's market. Similarly, if your script is full of typographical and spelling errors, it's just another reason for script readers to bounce it. As with any rule, people will queue at your door to point out exceptions but there are very few. Take the common sense view that your script won't figure among the exceptions and ensure you get it right before you get it out there.

I'm not asking you to restrict your creativity, merely to adapt it to the market place. As Syd Field says, screenplay format is not difficult to learn. It's quite straightforward and allows you plenty of variation when you know the parameters. I find that experienced writers, particularly of novels, have the most trouble adjusting. They have to curb their penchant for long descriptive passages, simile, metaphor etc., and learn to edit ruthlessly. Screenwriting is a minimalist form - your task is to convey the maximum emotion using the minimum words.

Expectations

- Type on one side of white paper; A4 in the UK, 8½" x 11" letter size in the US. Double-sided copies are becoming accepted but it's a slow burn.
- Type using 12-point Courier or Courier New. This is the Law.
- Only include on the page what takes place on the screen - think visual.
- Always write in the present tense - all screen action takes place in the here and now, regardless of when it's set.
- Don't number scenes. This only happens in a final shooting script which is ready for filming.
- Number pages at the top right hand corner, except the title page, which is never numbered.
- Don't bind your script using curly plastic binders or any other fancy stationery. In the UK, two-hole punch and bend-back brass brads are fine. In the US, three-hole punch with brads is standard. Keep it simple.
- If you cover your script, only use plain card covers with nothing written on them. Avoid dayglo or computer graphics.

Title Page

The title page contains only the title, the author's name(s) and the author's contact details, or those of his representative. Place the title in caps, centred, about a third of the page down. Double space to 'by.' Double space again to your name, in upper and lower case. If your script is based on other people's ideas or work, this should be acknowledged on the next double spaced line. Place contact details (address and landline, plus mobile, email and website if applicable) so that the last line is at the foot of the page, tabbed as far to the right as the longest line allows. Don't justify.

Layout

Margins: left indent is set approx. 1½" in, right indent approx. 1". Text begins approx. 1½" from top and ends approx. 1½" from bottom.

Scripts always begin with FADE IN: at top left. Double space to your first SLUG LINE. Slug lines, aka scene headings, are in caps from left. The reader needs to know whether the scene is interior (INT.), or exterior (EXT.), the location (CARNABY STREET or WALK-IN FREEZER) and the time (DAY or NIGHT). If the scene begins inside and moves outside, or shows both interior and exterior detail, use INT./EXT. I like to use bold type for FADE IN: and slug lines.

Double space to your first piece of SCENE DESCRIPTION, aka blackstuff. This sets the scene before any dialogue or voice-over narration. It is written clearly and concisely in the present tense, *and pertains only to what is on screen*. Don't use blackstuff to describe characters' feelings and emotions - you must find a way to show them visually.

Most of what you need to know about script format is covered in the following examples, from the opening three pages of my own script *Come And Get It* (from an idea by myself and Steve Reynolds):

FADE IN:
INT. HARVEY'S BEDROOM - NIGHT

On a sumptuous king-size bed two naked bodies tangle and roll, reflected in a full-length MIRROR on the facing wall. An empty champagne bottle bounces as the rolling becomes RHYTHM. LOUD ROCK MUSIC plays over.

HARVEY, a stocky middle-aged man, opens his mouth wide in an ecstatic O as a young, lithe GIRL JACKHAMMERS away on top. Her long blonde hair WHIPLASHES everywhere, cascading over her face and FLAYING his chest. Her long pink-tipped fingers are vices on his wrists.

Somewhere in the room, a mobile phone RINGS. They don't notice. Harvey SPASMS and, throwing his head back, lets out a long HOWL before slowly sinking, as if all the air has been sucked out of him. The MUSIC dies. The RINGING stops.

The girl slumps onto him, hair in his face, back glistening with sweat, pink nails slowly SCORING the wall. They PANT together for a moment until she ROLLS gymnastically off him. His POV: moving from her hair down her back to her long legs as she pads to the door. She takes a robe and shrugs into it.

Create a picture using an economy of words. Be clear about what you want the reader to know (or not know), the point of the scene, character objectives, plus the tone, pace and style. If you're writing a sex scene, don't be coy about it - give the reader the full experience. Never leave anything to the imagination. Occasionally I still encounter 'They then make love' or 'Car chase ensues.' This is the kiss of death. Would the writers dare submit a novel with chunks missing? Your job is to show, not tell, the reader how the scene works visually. Also, one page of correctly formatted script equals one minute of screen time. If a sex scene lasts one minute, or a car chase lasts three, then they should run to one and three pages respectively.

Formal etiquette:

- When characters first appear, flag their NAME in caps.
- SOUNDS are highlighted in caps.
- You can capitalise 'ACTION' words for emphasis, but don't overdo it.
- Avoid using explicit camera directions; instead try to visualise the scene and convey it to the reader. Pick out details to suggest certain angles and describe dynamically to suggest movement. (I know that certain script extracts in this book include camera directions, but the conventional wisdom is to leave them out.)
- Break long paragraphs into sections to make them more readable.
- POV refers to action seen from a particular character's Point Of View.

Now we're ready for some dialogue. Place dialogue after description, never begin a scene with it. Double space to CHARACTER CUE, to denote speech. Place cue (character name) in caps, approx. 3½" from the edge, *not* centred. Then single space to DIALOGUE, in upper and lower case, placed approx. 2½" from the edge. Dialogue should continue on next line if longer than about 3". Double space again to the next character cue, or blackstuff.

Continuing:

```
Harvey flicks sweat from his brow and blows out his cheeks.

                    HARVEY
          Third time for luck?

                    GIRL
          I'm hungry.

                    HARVEY
          I'm not surprised.

She bends to gather up a pile of clothes and jogs O.S. Harvey
plumps the pillows, sits up, finds and thumbs a remote con-
trol. ROCK MUSIC blasts. He thumbs it again and the volume
LOWERS.
```

```
                    GIRL (O.S.)
         I have to go.

                    HARVEY
         Hey. What about food?

                    GIRL (O.S.)
         What about it?

                    HARVEY
         I'm hungry too, you know.

                    GIRL (O.S.)
         I'm not surprised.
```

Harvey's POV: she strides past the bed, a blouse halfway over
her head, and disappears O.S. He runs his fingers through his
hair and eyes her greedily.

```
                    HARVEY
         Well, let's get a takeaway.

                    GIRL (O.S.)
         Not today.
                    (beat)
         Next time.
```

Wearing a long dark coat and swinging a handbag, she skips
across the room without even a glance at him.

```
                    GIRL (CONTD.)
         Next time. Takeaway. More
         fucking. 'Bye.
```

Harvey glares as she flounces out the door.

```
                    HARVEY
                    (shouts)
         Ciao, baby. Come back if you
         change your mind--
                    (under his breath)
         Bitch.
```

- Keep dialogue short and to the point - thrust, parry, counter-thrust; argument,
  counter-argument. Questions are often answered with another question. The
  more action oriented, the less dialogue. Even character-oriented scripts
  should avoid too many large blocks of dialogue, or worse, monologues -
  break it up using action/scene description.
- CHARACTER DIRECTION (as in Harvey's last piece of dialogue above) is
  placed in parentheses approx. 3¼" from the edge, and kept to a minimum.
  Leave it to actors to decide how to play it, unless emphasising volume, flag-

ging one character directly addressing another in a group, or if the character means the opposite of what he says.
- Don't confuse character direction with description. Character actions (gesturing, drinking etc.) are always placed in the blackstuff.
- O.S. means Off-Screen - dialogue spoken by someone present but unseen, or sound coming from off-camera.
- When a character's dialogue is broken by blackstuff, use (Contd.) after their next character cue or cues until another character speaks.
- Don't hyphenate words from line to line, or from page to page.
- A (beat) refers to a significant pause within dialogue.

Continuing:

The front door SLAMS O.S. Harvey takes another remote control from the bedside. He examines it, grins and thumbs it at the large MIRROR. On the bedside table, a phone RINGS. He ignores it. The ANSWERPHONE cuts in with a shrill BEEP. A MAN'S VOICE nervously sounds.

> MAN'S VOICE (V.O.)
> Mr. Harvey, it's Slater.
> > (beat)
> Are you there?
> > (beat)
> Christ. It's about the deal.
> There are-- problems, and--

Harvey flicks out a hand and SNATCHES the phone.

> HARVEY
> Problems?

> SLATER (V.O.)
> Ah.
> > (beat)
> Look, I've spoken with Mr
> Morgan and we need to talk--

> HARVEY
> Better come over then.

> SLATER (V.O.)
> Oh, I'm not sure--

> HARVEY
> Half an hour.
> > (beat)
> Problems are easily solved--

66

                        SLATER (V.O.)
            Oh yes, I--

                        HARVEY
            --if we keep our heads.

He cuts off the call, and HAMMERS the receiver down. His face
is set like concrete.

                        HARVEY (CONTD.)
            Morgan. Bastard. I'll keep
            your fucking head in my
            freezer.

He lies back and closes his eyes. His fingers PLOUGH through
his hair.

                        HARVEY (CONTD.)
            Problems. Always problems.

The front door SLAMS again. Harvey opens his eyes and looks
toward the door, expression brightening.

                        HARVEY (CONTD.)
            Baby, that you?
                        (laughs)
            Who else?

He lifts a champagne flute from the bedside, places it against
his forehead, then takes a long draught.

                        HARVEY (CONTD.)
            Changed your mind. Good. I'm
            ravenous. Thai? No, I think
            Cantonese, don't you?

FOOTSTEPS sound on the stairs.

                        HARVEY (CONTD.)
            Don't get those mushroom
            shoots or whatever again, eh?

He settles back, dipping his tongue into the flute. The door
slowly SWINGS open. He grins.

                        HARVEY (CONTD.)
            I don't know how you can eat—

His eyes WIDEN. A leather-gloved hand holds a GUN to his face.
The barrel has a SILENCER. The index finger FLEXES. The champagne flute EXPLODES.

                                                    CUT TO:

- V.O. means Voice-Over - narration or interior dialogue that is non-diegetic (unheard by the characters), or diegetic sound that is not necessarily off-screen, like Slater's answerphone message.
- Other abbreviations include: f.g. (foreground), b.g. (background), CU (close-up), LS (long shot), M.O.S. (soundless). Generally, avoid. Familiarise yourself with terms in the glossary at the end of the book.
- You can use a double dash (--) or ellipse (...) to indicate interrupted dialogue, or an occasional shorter pause.
- CUT TO: is a transition between scenes. A scene changes whenever there is a shift in time and/or location. It's your choice whether or not to use it.
- If you have to break dialogue from one page to the next, place (more) at the character cue, single-spaced from your last line of dialogue. Retype the character cue at the top of the next page, followed by (Contd.) A tip - only do this when your script is finished. Never break a sentence onto the next page, in dialogue or scene description.
- When continuing a scene onto the next page, you can type (CONTINUED) at the last right tab or justified right, double spaced from the last line of dialogue or scene description. At top left of the following page, type CONTINUED: and double-space to next line. Again, only do this when the script is finished, and its value is debatable.
- If you want to include a rapid series of images, type MONTAGE: in caps at left, and either number or bullet-point each image in sequence.
- Although you should avoid camera directions, I tend to direct the reader's imagination to specific details or framing by using ANGLE ON:

```
Slater appears in the bedroom doorway. Nervous, middle-aged,
wearing thick-rimmed glasses and an ill-fitting suit. Perspi-
ration glistens on his porcine face.

                    SLATER
          Mr Harvey?

ANGLE ON: Slater's face in f.g. with Harvey's body in b.g. A
droplet of sweat hangs precariously from the end of Slater's
nose as he steps into the room. His face contorts in HORROR as
his hands FLY to his mouth, his throat spasms in an involun-
tary RETCH, and he pitches forward, eyes rolling, trying to
fight nausea. Harvey's ruined crimson visage stares mutely up
at him.
```

Templates

Screenwriting software packages usually include formatting templates; Final Draft, Screenwriter 2000 etc. are available from The Screenwriter's Store (contact details in References & Notes chapter). They're all very good, but if you don't want to spend the money a freeware template I've used and can recommend is *SWiFT 97* (ScreenWriters' International Formatting Template for Word 97), which can be downloaded from www.impactpc.freeserve.co.uk.

Another very good, cheap alternative to the 'majors' is ScreenForge, which costs a registration fee of $45. It's available from www.apotheosispictures.com/.

8. Synopses, Outlines & Treatments

"You will write reams of treatments in your stay in Hollywood. And not a single word of them will be of any value to anyone. And still, you'll have to do them anyway."

Terry Rossio (Screenwriter)

Problems Of Semantics

These three terms present the novice Screenwriter with a headache, arising from their interchangeability of meaning; one person's Treatment is another's Outline, is yet another's Synopsis. There are many suggested functions and lengths for each form. I will therefore offer my interpretation of the terms; how I define them to navigate my own weary path through the minefield.

Synopses

I use a synopsis to commit the skeleton of the story to paper, right at the outset - the basic beginning, middle and end written in as close to one page of single-spaced A4 as possible. At this stage, it is little more than an exercise to list the major story events in chronological order. A synopsis is a document I use to help clarify my ideas. When you have worked out the main story events, write a linear synopsis to assist you in holding the full picture in your mind. Remember, as your story evolves, these events will change. Don't spend too much time rewriting the synopsis to reflect these changes because it takes precious time away from the script. When your story has its full complement of incidents write a 'final' synopsis, again keeping as close to a single page as you can.

Outlines

When you are confident you have identified all the major story events, you may find the outline, or step-outline, is a useful tool to co-develop story and plot. This is a method of outlining the bare bones of each scene on 5"×3" or 6"×4" lined index cards. The bare bones consist of: the slug line, characters present and a brief description of the action. The general rule is, if you can't fit the description on one side of the card, the scene may be too long and you should consider breaking it down. It's a good idea to write in pencil, as your scenes will evolve. Number your cards, again in pencil. The average length of a feature film scene is around two minutes, so 50-60 scenes/cards give you the skeleton of a feature script (remember, a scene change occurs whenever there is a change of location and/or time). Don't worry too much if you have lots of short scenes totalling more than 60 cards. This can be a good thing, especially in fast-paced action scripts; American films average nearly twice as many scenes as British or European films. Find a large wall or floor space where you can experiment with the order of your scenes to develop your plot - even if you think it will run chronologically, you may want to play around with sub-plots. Like the synopsis, the step-outline is for the writer's benefit and offers a user-friendly way to juggle events and arrive at the best dramatic framework for the plot.

Treatments

A treatment is usually written either when the story events are almost complete and require a more expanded and detailed document than a synopsis, or when the final draft script is ready for marketing. Writing an early treatment is advisable; it helps you to work out plot problems before attempting your first draft.

Although a treatment is excellent for getting a grip on the complexity of the plot and clarifying your thoughts, it is primarily a selling document to market yourself and your product. Increasingly, producers and agents are asking to read treatments. They can tell from the treatment whether or not the script (and the writer) will interest them, and it takes less time to read. The upside for the writer is that very good treatments open a lot of important doors; the downside is they may later discover they're better at writing treatments than they are at writing scripts and their beloved project may be passed to someone else.

Treatments should be regarded as an addition to a script, never as a replacement. Ultimately, no matter how good your treatment, the quality of your script remains the most important criterion on which you will be judged.

The treatment comprehensively documents the major incidents of the plot. It is written in the present tense, single-spaced, and contains the five Ws and an H: who, what, where, when, why and how; including (importantly) the end. The style should be pared down, flowing and entertaining to the reader. Broad strokes, no confusion or ambiguity, conveying the emotional impact of the story. There is little consensus on an ideal length, although anything over five pages is generally accepted as a treatment. Thirty- or even sixty-page treatments are not unheard of, but such a level of detail is unnecessary and seems to defeat the object of providing agents and producers with a short selling document. The time would be better spent developing your script. I try to work to a minimum of five pages and a maximum of twelve.

Julian Friedmann, who in his capacity as an agent has read thousands of treatments, advises writers to augment them to create the best impression. His four-part strategy contains a short (5-20 lines) introductory statement giving the premise, central character and key dramatic incident; 5-20 line biographies of the main characters; a statement of intent as to why the project is special for you, and you for it, and then the storyline as above. His suggested length is 10-20 pages.

Finding examples of treatments is notoriously difficult. Even Terry Rossio & Ted Elliott, in-demand screenwriters whose credits include *The Mask Of Zorro*,

Small Soldiers and *Shrek*, have said they get around having to produce treatments by asking execs for examples that they liked, knowing none will be forthcoming. There is an entertaining piece on treatments, including a few of their own, on their excellent website www.wordplayer.com.

I strongly suggest you develop a detailed plot treatment, including your act watersheds, focus points and mid-point, before you attempt your first draft. For further information try this site: www.writingtreatments.com.

9. Drafts

"...an author is one who can judge his own stuff's worth, without pity, and destroy most of it."

Colette (Author)

"Write from your heart; rewrite from your head"

Viki King (Screenwriting Lecturer)

First Draft

Remember that nothing good is ever written, it's *re*written. Through the pre-writing stage you've scribbled thousands of words working out ideas, research-ing, building character biographies, trying possible story directions, potential plot formations, whole unused scenes... and not one word has been wasted. You can't edit what you haven't written and you can't rework or build on what doesn't exist. For everything I complete, I expect to throw away the same amount of material if not more.

Now it's time for you to embark on the next phase - collating a few months' worth of notes, character biogs, plot points, scenes, sequences, synopses and treatments together into a first draft script. You should already have a good idea of the order of your plot events. They may change, and almost certainly will, but you can construct your first draft using the 7-point scaffolding: Opening Sequence, Act I Watershed, 1st Focus Point, Mid-Point, 2nd Focus Point, Act II Watershed and Climax. If you're unclear about any of these events, their func-tion in the plot, their connection to the other key events or to the protagonist's problems/tasks, then I'd advise you to delay your first draft until you have it all worked out.

The best way to approach your first draft is to aim to complete it as quickly as possible. Let it all come out. It will be loose and very weak in places. The dia-logue will be functional but unmemorable. The characters will seem sketchy, the plot unwieldy. Don't worry, this is all to be expected - these problems are all fixed in the redrafts. If you write five pages per day, it will be finished in a month. When you type **FADE OUT**. you can breathe a huge sigh of relief... for a short while.

Counterfeit

You've written your first draft screenplay. Fine. You're on track - but don't get carried away. You now have 90-120 pages of what looks, feels and reads like a script, but it is *not* a script. Until you complete its development it is a *counter-feit* script. If it progresses through several careful rewrites, the chances are you will have what looks, feels and reads like a good script. And this one really *is* a script, with a decent chance of finding a niche in the big cruel world. If you've been able to add originality, artistry and personality to the craft, you will have a great script, and people with chequebooks will beat a path to your door.

Now I really don't want to build you up only to bring you down, but this scenario is unlikely. Many writers produce a first draft that never goes any further, others lose interest during the redrafting stage, still others self-destruct somewhere else along the line. Robert McKee promises that your love of your script and yourself will wither and die long before you finish. Writing a screenplay is an endurance race akin to a marathon; you must be prepared for the long haul, no matter how punishing. Set yourself the goal of confounding statistics and do whatever you have to do to ensure your script is as good as it can be, *with the knowledge you possess at the time*. Your writing can only get better and your knowledge can only increase. Researching the market and developing your skills will pay dividends sooner or later. You may not achieve an outright script sale but you may find you possess another commodity that secures your first foothold in the industry - yourself. You could be taken on by an agent or asked to work on other material or to submit other material of your own. So before you knock on the igloo door make sure you have something that looks like a fridge.

Copyright

When you write anything substantial you should always copyright it. The essence of copyright is far simpler and less terrifying than many people think. Basically, you can't copyright ideas but you can copyright the work arising from them. As soon as you write something you automatically own its copyright. The more comprehensive the expression of your ideas, the more solid your copyright - it is better to copyright a treatment than a synopsis, for example.

Perhaps the cheapest and most effective way to establish it as your work is to mail it to yourself by registered post. The registration is proof of date, and the stamp is proof of a sealed envelope. I do this for prose stories, poems, treatments, first drafts and 'final' drafts. Don't send computer disks - hard copies can't corrupt. Sending work to a recognised third party is an additional protection. Your solicitor or bank should be happy to help. Certain organisations also offer copyrighting services - the Writers Guild Of America, US Copyright Office, UK Copyright Office, National Copyright Archive, Raindance, BECTU, PACT and some regional arts bodies.

Don't invite trouble; keep your work to yourself until it's finished and don't discuss your ideas with everyone you meet. Although you will be asked to sign disclaimer forms when you submit your work, don't get paranoid. The risk of being plagiarised or ripped off is minimal. If you have plagiarised someone else's work, the truth will out through the other party's copyright. If only your idea is similar there is no case to answer. Even if the scripts contain many parallels, you have your own chain of copyright to prove the history of your work.

Remember, ideas cannot be copyrighted precisely because of the similarity of many ideas in circulation at any one time. Anyway, as Wilson Mizner said, "If you steal from one author, it's plagiarism; if you steal from many, it's research."

Rewriting

The first thing to do after finishing your first draft (apart from copyrighting it) is to go and have some fun. Take a complete break; throw it in your desk drawer and leave it for a couple of weeks. Try not to think about it at all. *Don't* be tempted to rush out and show it to friends and family. The fact is, there's a lot wrong with it at this stage and although friends may not know exactly what its faults are, they'll realise they exist. Then their dilemma will be what to tell you. And because they like you, they'll tell you they love it. Never ask anyone to read anything that you know can be improved.

After your break, you'll return to your script with a fresh mind and a new impetus. To authenticate your counterfeit script, you have to take it through a series of careful rewrites, being specific about what you're focusing on each time. I'm a firm believer in a six-stage rewriting process, based on one suggested by Ray Frensham in his excellent book, *Teach Yourself Screenwriting*:

1. Coherence: Read your draft in one sitting, objectively, without taking notes. Is it coherent to someone who has never read it? Does it make sense? Does it hang together? Does each effect have a cause and does the reader always know why incidents happen or characters act? Are you foreshadowing major events and setting up your pay-offs (or paying off your set-ups?) Read it through once more and make notes on the problems and faults you encounter. Even if other faults leap out at you, unless they're directly concerned with coherence, leave them for later. When you've noted all of the problem areas, sit down and painstakingly repair them.

2. Structure & Plot: You began (or should have begun) your draft with seven key structural pillars in place. Rewriting is much more than joining the dots but the dots must still be there. Reread your draft, concentrating only on structure, and then rework to put everything in its right place. Your step-outline cards may be useful here. Do you regularly cut between plot and sub-plot? Do your sub-plots connect with and channel into the protagonist's plot line? Are you doing the right things at the right points on your timeline? Does your opening sequence hit the ground running, introduce the main characters, supply an intriguing inciting incident, set tone and pace? Are your watershed events powerful enough? Is your mid-point one from which there is no going back? Do your focus points loop around and tighten the plot and the protagonist's trajectories? Do you build conflict and accelerate the pace in act II, or does it slow and sag? Is your ending climactic? Structure is there to help you, but don't be afraid to knowingly work against it if you feel confident enough.

3. Character: Having written comprehensive biogs for your main characters, you should know them pretty well. Are they three-dimensional? Engaging? Empathetic? Are they original, with a life of their own, or are they 2-D facets of you? Do they have enough at stake in either normal or special world? Do you push them to extremes and place them in jeopardy? Are they active? Redraft to build their presence, vitality and uniqueness.

4. Visuals & Dialogue: Always ensure your story is told visually. What's on the page is what's on the screen, so give the reader visual information using dynamic language - strong verbs, unusual adjectives. Don't write 'goes' or 'gives' - find alternatives. Don't give explicit camera directions but do lead the reader's eye. Rather than write 'ECU of Morgan's eyes,' try 'Morgan's eyes BLAZE,' or 'Morgan's gaze BURNS into Jay's eyes.' Paint a picture. Ask questions about each line of dialogue. Does it further the plot and/or character? Is it memorable? Can you edit it? Can you remove it and accomplish the same thing visually? Is it too obvious? Too obscure? Does it sound like the character is speaking with his own voice or with yours? Establishing the visual identity for your script goes hand in glove with tightening and excising large chunks of dialogue.

5. Emotion & Style: Is your script in any way original? Is your own voice discernible and is it unique? Are you conveying a powerful theme to an audience or talking to yourself? Are you at least trying to put a new spin on old material? Do you have a consistent sense of your *mise en scène*; can you visualise the film in your mind? Do you include symbolism and subtext to enhance the richness of the story world? Do you constantly surprise the reader and reverse expectations? Do your scenes connect with each other and your overall concept? Can the reader find evidence of a unified vision? Are you creating tension and conflict but also humour and pathos? The style rewrite is crucial in formulating a priceless individual identity for your script.

Second Opinions

Whew! After reaching your fifth draft, you may be forgiven for never wanting to set eyes on your script again. The good news is, another break is at hand. Now is the time to seek other people's input.

Copyright it again. Then contact five people whose opinions you trust, tell them you've written a feature film screenplay and ask if they will read and respond to your work. If you can't think of five, try three. The more informed they are about films, the better. Impress upon them that you want an honest response and you want it within a month. If they agree, then email or post your script (with sae for return) immediately. Also include a set of questions based on the rewrites: did they understand it, what did they think of the characters/story/ dialogue etc. Encourage them to make additional comments. Final question: Did you like it/would you watch the film of it if it wasn't my script? Remember, they may not know too much about screenwriting, but they'll know what they like and dislike, and that's what counts.

You can now take your mind off your endeavours of the past few months. Party. Decorate. Have a holiday. Start researching and developing another script (brownie points if you do). When all of the responses are returned, sit down and read the script once more. Then read the comments - all of them, without emotion. Don't boil over if you read something scathing. Once you've read them, reread slowly and make notes. Are there any recurring comments? If they all make similar criticisms you'll need to act on them. List the points you agree/disagree with. Again, be objective and don't treat their comments as gospel. When you complete your notes, take stock of the situation. How many of the five liked your script? A solid thumbs-up from two is encouraging - 40% positive responses across the board from within the industry will see your work appreciated by a lot of important people. That said, almost all of these people will reject your script for any of a million reasons but even if it only earmarks you as someone to watch, that's a good thing.

Final Polish

In truth, there shouldn't be too many faults with your script after five careful redrafts, so the polish, which is the sixth stage of the rewriting process, should be mainly cosmetic. Work from your notes on the five responses and address *all* problems. Never knowingly allow faults to exist unrepaired. Work on every line, nuance, action, gesture, until they're exactly how you want them and you're sure that this is the best work you can possibly do at this time.

You may want to solicit professional opinion at this point. You're so close to the material that you may be blind to some of its flaws. A script appraisal costs around £50-75 and for that you'll get a 6-10 page report outlining strengths and weaknesses from someone who knows the industry's requirements. They should complete it in a couple of weeks or so. You must pay close attention to every point and be prepared to put in more work on any weaknesses they highlight. Do not put this off - the longer you leave it, the more apathetic about it you'll become.

And then, once you've reached **FADE OUT.** knowing you're not going to have to scan the whole thing microscopically again... congratulations. You can be genuinely proud. You have written a Feature Film script. You've manufactured your product and you're as confident as you can be of its quality. Copyright it, then go out and celebrate. When you sober up you'll probably feel a little deflated because you'll realise that you're about to embark on the next ridiculously difficult part of the process - trying to sell it.

10. Marketing

"The reality is that most scripts are not accessible enough because the writers, agents, script editors, development executives and producers are too complacent, too unambitious and in too much of a hurry."

Julian Friedmann (Agent)

"Money's better than poverty, if only for financial reasons."

Woody Allen (Screenwriter/Director/Actor)

Selling Yourself

After completing your redrafted and polished screenplay, you should be conscious of your achievement. If you've followed each step of the process and produced a script with an interesting premise, resonant theme, clever and coherent plot, three-dimensional characters, memorable dialogue, plenty of action and incident, without obvious flaws, *that is the best work you can produce at this stage of your knowledge*, then in truth you've accomplished something that proportionately few people who set out to write a screenplay ever manage.

So well done... you've made it halfway.

From this point on, you must concentrate on marketing a dual commodity - your work and its author. To sell a script you must sell yourself. The film industry depends on co-operation. With hundreds of people involved in each production, film-making is a highly collaborative medium which requires people to work together for a common goal. You can't be a loner; you must connect on a professional level with producers, agents, directors, financiers, actors etc. And, for a screenwriter, working on a professional level means being prepared to let your screenplay go when the cheque clears your bank; after all, when you sell a car you don't get to keep driving it.

Although you may feel your screenplay is finished, in the market place it remains a work in progress. No script is ever finished until the cameras roll, and often not even then. It is, as many have said, merely a blueprint for a film and it will go through significant changes as different opinions are sought and/or given. If you accept this, you may become involved in the post-sale rewriting process yourself. If you kick against it, or you're just unlucky, your work may be rewritten by other people. And if this should happen, then go out and celebrate again anyway, because your work is probably about to become a piece of celluloid history. From now on, you have no control over whether it shines like the sun or steams on the sidewalk; however, you've been paid and when you've sold once, you can sell again.

UK & US Markets

America and Britain are, as the maxim goes, two nations separated by a common language. This may be true but we are also separated by the gulf in our schmoozing ability. It's all down to a massive difference in attitude. Americans have a natural talent for selling themselves. They're comfortable with the idea of doing anything to succeed, including a lot of what British elitist thinking regards as false and over the top, but is absolutely necessary. You can't exist in LA without networking, doing brunch, shaking hands, sucking face, kissing ass, hanging out and hanging in with hundreds of people, all with one thing in common - in whatever way, they can help move your project forward. We Brits, on the other hand, tend to be more retiring, reserved and reticent about going after the money and contacts we need. We like to think that once the script is written, it will somehow sell itself. We're totally unprepared for pitching and we abhor the idea of diving into the market alongside our work. You need to ditch your hang-ups and court the industry. It won't come to you.

The key, whichever market you are aiming for, is to be professional. Research the industry, learn the craft of storytelling and gain the knowledge to feel comfortable in any environment. If you want to sell to the UK market, realise that most of the work is in TV and that opportunity in film is very limited. UK producers want character-based (in practice, often televisual) scripts that propagate a concept of 'Britishness' to sell at home and abroad, either broadly (class/history/military oriented) or specifically (regional/cultural). Most recent UK films fit this framework. If you want to sell to the US market, familiarise yourself with telling a dynamic story visually and economically, learn structure, action and genre and remember to make it appealing to 15-year-old males. You should also consider visiting Los Angeles to develop a feel for the place. It has its critics but it's deeply infused with its own magic and that of the movies. What's to fear, unless you're allergic to sunshine, palm trees or driving? If none of this interests you, then the best advice I can offer is: write about something that does interest you, passionately; make it cinematic and so damn good that neither market can turn it down.

Approaching The Business: Agents

You need to introduce your script and yourself to the business. Specifically, those elements within the industry who are there to deal with writers and their quirky but maybe brilliant brains. Some people within the top echelon of the industry still haven't shaken off the notion that it is an exclusive club for the furtherance of their interests, and breaking down the door is hard. Gatekeepers are everywhere, so the ideal element to target is the one that will bypass them and allow you into at least the smoking rooms. These elements are agents and, true to the Catch-22 nature of the business, they are difficult for spec screenwriters to obtain.

With many production companies no longer accepting unsolicited material, having an agent opens up a route that the industry had almost closed off. Agents are invaluable because of their experience in selling writers' work, dealing with legal matters and their vast web of contacts. Unfortunately, many agents no longer take on new writers and those that do naturally devote most of their time to their existing clients, 10-15% of whose earnings provides their living. They receive thousands of enquiries from first-time writers every year, and simply don't have the resources to deal with them all. Sooner or later you'll need an agent, so when you write a script you are proud of, don't waste any opportunity to get it into the shop window.

Consult the *Writers & Artists' Yearbook* for a list of UK agencies and phone them to find which ones accept spec material. Never ask to speak to an agent but do get the name of the person you should contact. Never send scripts; always approach using a clear, concise, professional enquiry letter. The letter should include:

- A sentence or two about yourself; what you do, that you've written a feature script, then give the title and the genre.

- The paper pitch. Sell your script in three to five lines. Essentially, it's a story about a character (reformed hitman, guilty priest etc.) who wants to achieve/ complete (main goal/task), but is prevented by (force of antagonism or main outer problem), complicated by (fear/ghost/nemesis), until finally (how it all ends - state this creatively to intrigue them).

- A closing sentence saying you are seeking representation and that you look forward to their reply.

This letter is the correct protocol for approaching agents, producers or anyone in a position to progress your work. Maybe (I'm tempted to write 'probably') you'll receive a reply saying thanks but no thanks, but maybe you'll receive a reply asking you to submit the script. They may also require a short synopsis and/or treatment, and a CV. I hope it goes without saying that whatever they ask for, make sure you provide.

If they don't want your script, you may have to chase them to return it - but if you haven't included a sae, they won't. Give them a month before making a polite enquiry call. If they send a letter of rejection, they may not go into reasons. If you want to know why, call them. They may be too busy to talk to you but you're entitled to ask.

If they like your script, they'll ask for a meeting. Be polite, professional and prepared to discuss your work objectively. If they like you and your work, they may take you on. They will start to tout your script right away, or suggest improvements beforehand, and foster a career plan with you to keep you producing good material. Only through writing a high-quality script can you expect to jump any industry hurdle, however small.

Other Business

The other organisations to approach are production companies, national and regional development agencies, funding bodies; again, anyone who can progress your work in any way. Try Production Companies and Independents (*Screen International* has a January round-up of all UK productions with company contact details; *The Knowledge* contains almost every contact in the business), Film-Four, BBC, BSkyB, EMDA, The Film Council and its subsidiaries, Television Companies - be thorough in your research. Join organisations like Raindance, the New Producer's Alliance and the Screenwriter's Workshop. Enter screenwriting competitions and attend workshops. Subscribe to magazines, get on mailing lists and e-newsletters, always look for new contacts and information. For a spec screenwriter, the term 'Media Whore' is not an insult, it's a compliment - but only if you have a script that's good enough.

Pitching

The most fearsome necessary evil for a writer is the script pitch, where you literally sit or stand in front of someone with the clout to take your project on board and sell them what it's about. Not tell, sell. In as few words as possible, as you'll have very little time. Ten minutes is luxury. This is the stage (in both senses of the word) where you really do sell yourself - plenty of good scripts are rejected because the writer can't pitch to save his life. Needless to say, Americans tend to be better than Brits.

- Practice makes perfect, so rehearse your pitch, over and over. Confidence is vital. Don't be overawed or tongue-tied.
- Know your script well enough to field any question from any angle.
- Know its marketability. If it is high concept and has unique selling points, you have a head start.
- Prepare a log-line. This is a disposable hook that just might stick. You've seen them many times - 'In Space, No One Can Hear You Scream' (*Alien*) etc.
- Know the people you're pitching to. Do your homework on them.
- Give the three- to five-line pitch, then embellish.
- Be passionate about your material, but not to the point of frightening them.
- On the other hand, being boring is the cardinal sin of pitching.
- Have other pitches up your sleeve in case it goes well.

In Britain, you'll know how it's going from the reaction. If it goes very badly, just get up and politely exit. If it goes well, be attentive, humble and, yes, professional. If they like you and your script, you have just hurdled one of your own largest obstacles.

Be careful not to get too excited if you're pitching in LA - everyone will be nice to you. William Goldman's catchphrase, "Nobody knows anything," applies. They may think you're a klutz but they won't say so. Appearances can be deceptive and you might have the Next Big Thing in your bag, maybe not this time but the next. And because so many jobs are so precarious, very few people can afford opinions.

When writer/director Stuart Gordon was in London filming *Space Truckers*, he told the following story: after coming up with the idea for the successful *Honey, I Shrunk The Kids* he was given an office on the Disney backlot. Some time later he pitched a story idea to an executive and, after an encouraging response, left a treatment. The exec said he'd get back to him very soon. Weeks passed without contact. One lunchtime they happened to meet in a restaurant and Stuart asked if he had liked the treatment. Sheepishly, the man replied, "I don't know; no one else has read it yet."

LA is a great place if you can divorce emotion from business but a dangerous one if you're looking to forge beautiful friendships with creative and talented people. In F Scott Fitzgerald's *The Last Tycoon*, fictional studio boss Monroe Stahr is asked if he likes the movie business. He replies, "Sure. Sure I like it. It's nice being the only sound nut in a hatful of cracked ones." The irony is, in Hollywood every exec thinks he's the only sound nut for miles around.

Deals

There are a million possible deals that can be made for the outright sale, partial sale, option or lease of your work, and no space to go into them in detail here. Suffice to say, don't get ripped off. If you have an agent, let them take care of the contracts after you've consulted on offers that will be acceptable to you. If you don't have an agent, get an experienced media contracts lawyer and either pay by the hour or agree a percentage (usually much less than an agent's). If you try to handle the negotiations yourself, you'll almost certainly wish you hadn't.

You may be asked to rewrite your script, to write or rewrite a treatment, to rewrite someone else's script etc. All of these activities come with remuneration. Never work for free. In the USA, the Writers Guild operates statutory legal minimum rates; scandalously, in the UK these rates are merely 'suggested.' We all know what 'suggested' means. Currently, the UK rates are around £23,000 for features with a budget of £2m+, and £14,000 for features budgeted under £2m. The US rates are around the $90,000 and $50,000 marks, are legally-enforceable floors and of course scripts are sold every day in LA for mid-to-high six-figure sums, or more. The US market works because of its best efforts. The UK market works, if it works (and as you'll probably have gathered, I have my reservations), despite its best efforts but let that only serve as further motivation.

Best Wishes

If you dedicate yourself, for one year of your life, to creating a great script and you actually manage to do it, you will be a fulfilled and wealthier person for having done so and not a little extraordinary. You will also have gained a precious foothold in an industry notorious for its refusal to admit new members. If this book or others like it helps you in any way to achieve a sale, then my efforts to fit five hundred-plus pages of screenwriting theory into a hundred will not have been a waste of time.

Good luck.

11. Troubleshooting

"You can be a wonderful doctor, but unless you learn certain surgical techniques, you may kill a lot of people."

Mike Figgis (Writer/Director)

Self-Diagnosis

Sorting the shit from the shinola is a talent every writer needs but few do it well, either through lack of objectivity, or knowledge of how to go about it, or both. Writers constantly argue the merits of lost causes and dead ends within their scripts, straining to shoehorn them into an unyielding framework because they're so in love with their ideas, or they really think it all fits together. Writing, particularly scriptwriting, is all about murdering your loved ones in the service of greater causes - drama and plot. Get used to it and get over yourself.

Script Appraisals

It helps if you know what script readers are looking for before you submit your work for consideration. If you have doubts (and you probably should), consider investing in a script appraisal. As I said, a 6-10 page report costs around £50-£75 but you'll usually find it's money well spent. I use the following appraisal checklist:
- Is it clear?
- Focused?
- Well structured?
- Written with style?
- Concept intriguing?
- Marketable?
- Cinematic or televisual?
- For what audience?
- Where does attention wane?
- Is protagonist dynamic/sympathetic?
- Clear needs/wants/goals/problems?
- Character development/interaction?
- Enough tension/conflict?
- Memorable dialogue?
- Twists and switches?
- Strong ending?
- What has protagonist learned?
- What works?
- What stinks?
- Conclusion

These points are broadly similar to those addressed by script readers and they also serve as useful guidelines when redrafting. A tip: complete your script to the best of your ability before having it appraised. If you know it has flaws, why pay to have someone else tell you? Virtually all scripts I read share common problems which could have been avoided by research and preparation. Many are covered in earlier chapters but a new perspective is always useful, so I asked two people with plenty of script-reading expertise to discuss some of the problems they encounter time and again:

Charles Harris

Charles Harris is a writer, director, script editor, reader and doctor. His debut feature as writer/director, *Paradise Grove*, was completed earlier this year. He is co-chair of the New Producers' Alliance (NPA) and a founder-member of the London Screenwriter's Workshop (now Screenwriter's Workshop (SW)). Charles also teaches at the SW and at the London Film School.

Ten Common Problems

1. Most scripts do not have a sense of the audience/reader. They're not speaking to, or engaging the reader; there's no sense of who it's being aimed at or made for. Also, they're not written in such a way you feel the audience will 'get it' - there's no sense of clear purpose, no sense the reader feels communicated with. It's down to a basic problem of communication and this first problem encapsulates all of the other variations.

2. There's no personality coming through. It doesn't matter whether the script is well crafted, the writer has just spent time solving problems at the expense of personality. It's anonymous. Again, this is a problem of engagement.

3. There's no focused aim for the main character(s) - what do they want? There may be a vague feeling of a problem, like a marriage breakdown etc., but it's not focused. Writers fail to narrow the focus to the final part of the script that gets to the thing that solves the hero's problem.

4. Too long spent setting up. Characters spend a long time talking about problems but too little time doing anything about them.

5. Individual scenes tend to tell rather than show. They need to be more focused and have personality and style. There's no focusing down to the essence of the scene, so that we can be shown rather than told.

6. The writer doesn't spend long enough developing character. Characters are the heart of the script. They tend to be either too positive or too negative, not complex enough. Writers should consider themselves students of people.

7. Far too much talky dialogue. If characters are endlessly talking, how is the scene going to work visually?

8. Flat writing style. The writing style has to engage the reader. There are too many nouns and adjectives used, and nowhere near enough strong verbs.

9. No theme. What's the point of it if the reader can't discern a theme? Why do it at all?

10. No difference. Writers must ask themselves the question 'why is this different?' Too often it's just not in any way new. And if you know it's not new, then at least ask yourself 'what am I bringing to it?'

Ten Handy Hints

1. Make obstacles for your main character. Lots of little ones - toothache, lost hair grip etc. which must be resolved. Build obstacles to delay the satisfaction of the audience.

2. Write a treatment first. There is no definitive idea of what constitutes a treatment; the terms 'treatment,' 'outline' and 'synopsis' are interchangeable, although the longer it is, the more likely it is to be called a treatment. And you must give the ending! A treatment helps you to clarify your thoughts. It's difficult, but very important. Start with a short pitch of 25 words or less. Films make their money on TV and video. Make it saleable to TV and condensable to a short entry in the TV Times: Someone wants _____, but is prevented from getting it by _____. Then write a short synopsis giving the problem, how the protagonist goes about solving it and how it all ends up - the basic three acts. Elaborate and enlarge on that for the treatment. The treatment must be readable and must flow. Use conjunctions: moreover, meanwhile, on the other side of town and so on.

3. Format is very important. Think about it like a date: you prepare yourself by showering, grooming, dressing well, looking your best. You make the effort to show yourself in the best possible light. If you don't, your date will be unimpressed. It's the same with format. If your script format is wrong, your story may not have attention paid to it. And yes, you must use 12 point Courier. Format is vital, it's part of your marketing.

4. Write your first draft quickly, then rewrite slowly.

5. Put it aside for a few months. You need that distance. Or, have lots of people look at it. Show it to friends. Give them a list of questions - tell them to stop at page 40, then write down who is the main character, what do they want, what are their problems, how are they going about solving them? Find out if you are communicating with and engaging the reader.

6. Deal with every problem. There's no such thing as a problem you can sweep under the carpet. If there's a hint of a problem, it will be magnified throughout the process, and certainly found out by a reader.

7. When you've finished your script, find a producer or producers who seem to share your sensibility. Join organisations that can help you - the NPA and the SW, definitely.

8. Never send your script out cold; always use an approach letter, or a phone call.

9. Build relationships, network etc. Be a collaborator. The industry wants people they can work with. All scripts need rewriting. Compromises have to be made.

10. When you send out your scripts, use thick envelopes. It's amazing how many arrive tatty or shredded because the writer has used thin, flimsy envelopes. Padded envelopes are best.

Elliot Grove

Elliot Grove is a writer, director, producer and script reader. He wrote and directed the no-budget feature *Table Five* for just over £200, has produced three features and over fifty short films. He is the founder of Raindance, an independent training organisation based in London, providing training and resources for directors, producers and screenwriters. Out of this grew the Raindance Film Festival, the largest independent film festival in Europe, of which Elliot is Director. He is also the author of *Write + Sell The Hot Screenplay*.

Five Common Problems

1. Writing a story where the hero does not have clearly defined wants and needs. 95% of stories fail because of this.

2. Writing a story which is not commercially viable.

3. Presenting a screenplay in incorrect format.

4. Writing a story where there is no ghost or backstory, or writing a story where the hero overcomes the ghost too easily.

5. Writing a story containing characters the audience cannot identify with.

The core problems identified by Charles and Elliot will be familiar to all script readers. Use their advice and the following checklist to help diagnose and solve your script's problems.

Troubleshooting 10-Point Checklist

1. Does your protagonist have clearly defined motivations and goals: needs, desires, fears, ghost, problems? Have you communicated to the reader who the protagonist is, what he wants, how he plans to achieve his goals and what's standing in his way?

2. Do your characters exist in their own world as complex, three-dimensional, credible people with whom the reader can identify? If they're not alive in your mind they won't be alive in the reader's. What are their backstories? Do you know your characters well enough?

3. Who is your audience? What is the genre? How would you market the finished film? Does your script have commercial appeal, or an everyman quality? Do you know whether it's high-concept (with such a strong premise that audiences will go and see it for that reason alone), or low/soft-concept (depends more on the quality of the end product to attract its audience, and therefore more risky for financiers)? Why would anyone pay to watch this film? Why would anyone pay to fund this film?

4. What is the point of your script? What makes it different; what's worth the time, effort and paper? What is the theme - what is it really about? Are you communicating this effectively? Do you know yourself - could you state the theme as well as the premise if asked? Are you saying something because you're desperate to say it or because you think it's commercial?

5. Is your script coherent and integrated, or a Frankensteinian monster of loosely-assembled parts? Do you have enough ideas, characters and sub-plots to sustain a 90-120 page script? Have you paid enough attention to structure? Does your opening hit the ground running and hook the reader? What are your end-of-act plot points? Is there a mid-point? Does your ending deliver, and tie all the plot strands? Are you engaging the reader and holding interest throughout? Are you building tension, accelerating the pace, increasing the frequency and difficulty of obstacles your protagonist faces? Or does interest wane, the pace sag and the script run out of steam? Are you capable of objectivity when self-analysing?

6. Is your writing style stylish enough? Are you transmitting your story visually into the mind of the reader (showing), or indulging in bland reportage (telling)? Remember that in screenwriting, less is definitely more. Is your scene description pared down, fast paced and specific or meandering, hyperbolic and general?

7. Does your protagonist spend enough time in active pursuit of goals and solving problems or too much time talking? Readers engage with characters through actions first and dialogue a distant second. Is there enough at stake? Is your protagonist in enough danger? Is he on the edge? True character is revealed only in adversity. What does he stand to lose - a game of poker, a round of golf or loved ones, career, reputation, life? Is his goal difficult, plausible and important enough? Is the reader given a sense of gravitas or couldn't care less?

8. Have you laid out your script in the correct format? Is it too long or too short? Is it full of typos, spelling and/or grammatical errors, strange punctuation? These elements are not negotiable. Sending out a badly formatted or presented script is an excuse for a reader to put a cross against your name. It's a crime of stupidity. You may as well include your own pre-written rejection slip.

9. Have you remembered that scripts are about parallel action? Several things are happening to several people at once. Are you showing this by cutting back and forth between them, often? Are your scenes short and sweet enough to allow

the script to flow or do you concentrate on one character's plot line for too long at a time?

10. Does your script contain that synergy of concept, execution, character and incident that elevates it from a televisual to a cinematic experience? Would the film of your script cry out to be viewed in a cinema or would it lose nothing if shown on a TV screen? Have you gone to the extremes with your characters, situations and style? Is your canvas large enough, or is it television masquerading as film?

12. References & Notes

Books On Screenwriting

Screenplay: The Foundations Of Screenwriting (Third Edition) by Syd Field, US: Dell, 1994, Paperback, 262 pages, $13.95, ISBN 0440576474

The Screenwriter's Workbook by Syd Field, US: Dell, 1984, Paperback, 211 pages, $9.95, ISBN 0440582253

Story: Substance, Structure, Style And The Principles Of Screenwriting by Robert McKee, UK: Methuen, 1998, Hardback, 466 pages, £16.99, ISBN 0413715507

Writing Screenplays That Sell by Michael Hauge, UK: Elm Tree, 1989, Paperback, 316 pages, £11.99, ISBN 0241126827

Teach Yourself Screenwriting by Raymond G Frensham, UK: Hodder & Stoughton, 1996, Paperback, 250 pages, £6.99, ISBN 034060378X

Alternative Scriptwriting: Writing Beyond The Rules by Ken Dancyger & Jeff Rush, US: Focal Press, 1991, Paperback, 212 pages, $26.95, ISBN 0240800753

Screenwriting 434 by Lew Hunter, US: Perigee, 1993, Paperback, 351 pages, $13.95, ISBN 039951838

Making A Good Script Great by Linda Seger, US: Dodd, Mead & Company, Inc., 1987, Paperback, 204 pages, $8.95, ISBN 0396089534

Film Scriptwriting: A Practical Manual (Second Edition) by Dwight V Swain & Joye R Swain, US: Focal Press, 1988, Paperback, 422 pages, ISBN 0240511905

How To Make Money Scriptwriting (Second Edition) by Julian Friedmann, UK: Intellect, 2000, Paperback, 219 pages, ISBN 184150002X

The Complete Book Of Scriptwriting by J Michael Straczynski, US: Writer's Digest, 1996, Hardback, 424 pages, $21.99, ISBN 0898795125

How To Write A Movie In 21 Days: The Inner Movie Method by Viki King, US: Harper Perennial, 1988, Paperback, 192 pages, $11.00, ISBN 0062730665

Raindance Writers' Lab: Write + Sell The Hot Screenplay by Elliot Grove, UK: Focal Press, 2001, Paperback, 240 pages plus CD-ROM, £14.95, ISBN 0240516362

Other Books Of Interest

The Guerilla Film-Makers Handbook by Chris Jones & Genevieve Jolliffe, UK: Cassell, 1996, Paperback, 448 pages, ISBN 0304338540

Adventures In The Screen Trade by William Goldman, UK: Futura, 1990, Paperback, 418 pages, £5.99, ISBN 0708848826

Easy Riders, Raging Bulls by Peter Biskind, UK: Bloomsbury, 1998, Hardback, 506 pages, £20.00, ISBN 0747536309

A Pound Of Flesh by Art Linson, US: Avon, 1995, Paperback, 195 pages, $9.00, ISBN 0380724014

Stranger Than Paradise: Maverick Film-Makers In Recent American Cinema by Geoff Andrew, UK: Prion, 1998, Hardback, 374 pages, £16.99, ISBN 1853752746

Filming On A Microbudget by Paul Hardy, UK: Pocket Essentials, 2001, 96 pages, £3.99, ISBN 190304748X

Creative Writing by Neil Nixon, UK: Pocket Essentials, 2002, 96 pages, £3.99, ISBN 1904048099

Screenwriting Magazines

Script, $6.95 Bimonthly, 5638 Sweet Air Road, Baldwin, MD 21013-0007, USA. www.scriptmag.com

Creative Screenwriting, $6.95 Bimonthly, 6404 Hollywood Blvd, Suite 415, Los Angeles, CA 90028-6261, USA. www.creativescreenwriting.com

Scenario, $20 Quarterly, 104 Fifth Avenue, New York, NY 10011, USA. www.scenariomag.com

Scriptwriter - new UK magazine edited by agent Julian Friedmann. www.scriptwritermagazine.com

Other Magazines

Screen International, £2.50 Weekly, EMAP Media, 33-39 Bowling Green Lane, London EC1R 0DA, UK. www.screendaily.com

Filmmaker, $5.50 Quarterly, 110 West 57th Street, 3rd Floor, New York, NY 10019-3319, USA. www.filmmakermagazine.com

Empire, £2.80 Monthly, Seventh Floor, Endeavour House, 189 Shaftesbury Avenue, London WC2H 8JG, UK. www.empireonline.co.uk

Uncut, £3.50 Monthly, IPC Media, 24th Floor, King's Reach Tower, Stamford Street, London SE1 9LS, UK. www.uncut.net/index.html

Organisations

Raindance, 81 Berwick Street, London W1V 3PF, UK. Tel. 020 7287 3833, www.raindance.co.uk

First Film Foundation, 9 Bourlet Close, London W1W 7BP, UK. www.firstfilm.co.uk

New Producers Alliance, 9 Bourlet Close, London W1P 7PJ, UK. Tel 020 7580 2480, www.npa.org.uk

Euroscript, 1-8 Whitfield Place, London W1P 5SF, UK. Tel 020 7387 5880, www.euroscript.co.uk

Shooting People, www.shootingpeople.org

The Script Factory, www.scriptfactory.co.uk

Specialist Shops

Cinema Bookshop, 13-14 Great Russell Street, London W1, UK. Tel 020 7637 0206

The Screenwriters Store Ltd, Suite 121, Friars House, 157-168 Blackfriars Road, London SE1 8EZ, UK. Tel 020 7261 1908 www.thescreenwritersstore.co.uk

Other Websites

There are hundreds of 'em. Here are my favourites:

www.script-o-rama.com/snazzy/dircut.html - Script resource.

www.lsw.org - Screenwriter's Workshop website for UK news, events, workshops.

www.screen-lab.co.uk - UK courses, workshops, events.

www.nftsscreenwriting.org - National Film & TV School website.

www.xerif.com - Directory of all UK script competitions.

www.wga.org - Writers Guild Of America site.

www.scriptsales.com - Screenplays, pitches, treatments, books, latest sales.

www.wordplayer.com - Screenwriters Terry Rossio & Ted Elliott's wonderful site. Now they're in demand, I hope they finish their projected 60-column project. The collected columns would make the most entertaining screenwriting book yet.

www.moviebytes.com - Script competitions, agencies, news, chat, sales.

www.screenplay.com - Screenwriting software and downloadable demos.

www.writerswebsite.com - Scripts, resources.

www.screentalk.org - Good US magazine website.

www.screenwriter.com - Coverage, masterclasses by working screenwriters.

www.madscreenwriter.com - Resources, articles, entertaining.

www.euroscreenwriters.com - Articles and interviews on European film-makers.

www.finaldraft.com - The industry standard software package website.

www.screenwritersutopia.com - News, sales, market, workshops.

www.theknowledgeonline.com - Database of 15,600 companies and crew.

www.imdb.com - The place to go for film reference.

www.variety.com - Famous US trade magazine's even better website.

www.aint-it-cool-news.com - Harry Knowles' legendary geeksite.

www.netribution.com - News, reviews etc.

www.kamera.co.uk - News, reviews etc.

13. Glossary

I've tried to keep the text as jargon-free as possible, but there are a number of screenplay terms with which you should be familiar:

ACT - Feature scripts are normally structured in three acts, the second roughly twice the length of the first and third. Plot Points propel one act into the next. The first act is generally the set-up; the second the conflict, or the plot and the third the climax and resolution.

ACTOR DIRECTION - Parenthetical instruction to indicate how dialogue should be delivered inserted, single spaced, situated midway between Character Cue and Dialogue.

ANTAGONIST - The Bad Guy, or Villain. Function: to impede the Hero's progress towards his goal.

BACKSTORY - The significant, relevant events to have taken place in characters' lives prior to the point at which we meet them.

BEAT - A term normally used to denote a pause, usually for emphasis, placed single-spaced in parentheses between lines of dialogue. Confusingly, you may also find the term used to refer to beats within scenes, in a rhythmic sense.

b.g. - Screenplay form abbreviation for an event or action taking place in the background.

BLACKSTUFF - Scene Description.

CHARACTER ARC - The imaginary curve of a character as they progress through the script.

CHARACTER CUE - Character's first name in caps, placed 3½" from left, indicating character's dialogue which follows on the next line.

CLOSE-UP (C.U.) - Camera direction to suggest a frame-filling shot for emphasis, e.g. a hand holding a gun, an expression of shock etc. Use sparingly - remember, you are not the director.

COVERAGE - Written 'report' on scripts by script readers working for production companies etc.

CUT TO: - Term placed in caps at right of page, double spaced before and after, to emphasise the edit between the end of one scene and the beginning of the next. Some writers never use this; others use it all the time.

DIALOGUE - Characters' words. Minimise it, further characters with it and make it memorable.

DISSOLVE TO: - Similar to CUT, but suggesting a dissolve rather than a hard cut. Can be used to indicate a softer segue into a flashback or dream sequence. Like FADE or WIPE, avoid unless you have a cast-iron reason to use it.

DRAFT - A stage of a screenplay. First draft is your exploratory draft after completing your comprehensive notes and pre-writing.

EXPOSITION - Another term for backstory.

EXTERIOR (EXT.) - The first part of a scene heading (slug line), indicating an outdoor location. INTERIOR (INT.) is the flipside. INT./EXT. (or vice-versa) indicates a scene which has elements of both interior and exterior; action may move from one to the other, or may be shot through a window, or in a moving car.

EXTREME CLOSE-UP (E.C.U.) - Camera direction to suggest a frame-filling shot for emphasis, but more detailed than a close-up, e.g. the gun barrel, eyes widened in shock etc. Again, use very sparingly.

FADE IN - The first words of a screenplay, in caps, at left margin. Double space after.

FADE OUT - The last words of a screenplay, in caps, at right edge. Double space before.

FADE TO BLACK - Can you think of a good reason for it? No, neither can I. Watch *Dead Man* for a really irritating example.

f.g. - Screenplay form abbreviation for events or action taking place in the foreground.

FLASHBACK - A device used to alter the script's subjective timeline. A scene might flash back to a character's memory, an event that took place in the nineteenth century, or WW2, or a key incident informing the current stage of the plot.

FLASHFORWARD - As above, self-explanatory.

FREEZE FRAME - Command to arrest movement, stopping the timeline dead. Can be used to indicate a photograph being taken, or as a device to introduce flashbacks etc. More common to art film narratives, again to be avoided unless you can justify its use.

GENRE - French word meaning 'type.' Used as a convenient marketing shorthand by producers and consumers alike.

INCITING INCIDENT - The Big Event that sets up the narrative, and provides the protagonist with his problem. Can also mean a major plot point event.

LOG-LINE - Short, catchy line to sell the essence of your premise.

LONG SHOT (L.S.) - Camera shot of a character's entire body.

MEDIUM SHOT (M.S.) - Camera shot of a character's torso and head.

MISE EN SCENE - Literally, what is on the screen.

MONTAGE - Fast-edited series of shots, often used in set pieces.

OFF-SCREEN (O.S.) - Sound or dialogue taking place off-screen that we can hear but cannot see the cause of, or characters speaking.

PAY-OFF - Belated resolution to something set up earlier in the plot.

PLOT POINT - Watershed event, punching the plot into the next Act.

POINT OF VIEW (P.O.V.) - Subjective shot as if through a character's eyes.

PROTAGONIST - The Hero. Your main character, the focus of the plot.

SCENE - Unit of narrative time. Scene changes occur when there is a shift in time or location.

SCENE DESCRIPTION - The 'blackstuff' or stylised prose describing relevant details of each scene and setting up atmosphere, mood etc.

SET-UP - Can refer to the function of Act I or to foreshadowing certain details which will be paid off later.

SEQUENCE - A thematically-linked series of scenes.

SLUG LINES - Scene headings, INT., EXT. etc.

STEP OUTLINE - System using index cards (one per scene) to help order plot events.

STRUCTURE - The principle of telling stories using an underpinning framework; film narratives are often structured in three acts.

SUB-PLOT - Plot subordinate to the protagonist's outer actions; pertaining to his inner motivations or motivations of other characters.

SYNOPSIS - Single-page document telling the main story events in chronological order.

TREATMENT - More comprehensive document, usually around 5-12 pages, giving the major plot events or a more in-depth version of the story. A treatment of the finished script is used as a selling document complementing the script.

VOICE-OVER (V.O.) - Usually used for narration revealing a character's thoughts or a storytelling perspective from someone outside the narrative. Can also be used for taped or telephone voices.

WE SEE/WE HEAR - Try to avoid this device in your scene description.

WITHOUT SOUND (M.O.S.) - If, for whatever reason, the scene or part of it plays in silence - for example, two characters can be seen in long shot, but we can't hear them.

FADE OUT.

The Essential Library: Currently Available

Film Directors:

Woody Allen (2nd)	Tim Burton	Ang Lee
Jane Campion*	John Carpenter	Joel & Ethan Coen (2nd)
Jackie Chan	Steve Soderbergh	Clint Eastwood
David Cronenberg	Terry Gilliam*	Michael Mann
Alfred Hitchcock (2nd)	Krzysztof Kieslowski*	Roman Polanski
Stanley Kubrick (2nd)	Sergio Leone	Oliver Stone
David Lynch	Brian De Palma*	George Lucas
Sam Peckinpah*	Ridley Scott (2nd)	James Cameron
Orson Welles (2nd)	Billy Wilder	
Steven Spielberg	Mike Hodges	

Film Genres:

Blaxploitation Films	Bollywood	French New Wave
Horror Films	Spaghetti Westerns	Vietnam War Movies
Vampire Films*	Heroic Bloodshed*	
Slasher Movies	Film Noir	

Film Subjects:

Laurel & Hardy	Marx Brothers	Film Music
Steve McQueen*	Marilyn Monroe	The Oscars®
Filming On A Microbudget	Bruce Lee	Writing A Screenplay

TV:

Doctor Who

Literature:

Cyberpunk	Philip K Dick	The Beat Generation
Agatha Christie	Sherlock Holmes	Noir Fiction*
Terry Pratchett	Hitchhiker's Guide (2nd)	Alan Moore

Ideas:

Conspiracy Theories	Nietzsche	UFOs
Feminism	Freud & Psychoanalysis	Bisexuality

History:

Alchemy & Alchemists	The Crusades	The Black Death
Jack The Ripper	The Rise Of New Labour	Ancient Greece
American Civil War	American Indian Wars	

Miscellaneous:

The Madchester Scene	Stock Market Essentials	Beastie Boys
How To Succeed As A Sports Agent		

Available at all good bookstores or send a cheque (payable to 'Oldcastle Books') to: **Pocket Essentials (Dept WAS), 18 Coleswood Rd, Harpenden, Herts, AL5 1EQ, UK.** £3.99 each (£2.99 if marked with an *) . For each book add 50p postage & packing in the UK and £1 elsewhere.